CW01283860

IDI AMIN

Lion of Africa

Manzoor Moghal

authorHOUSE®

AuthorHouse™ UK Ltd.
500 Avebury Boulevard
Central Milton Keynes, MK9 2BE
www.authorhouse.co.uk
Phone: 08001974150

© 2010 Manzoor Moghal. All rights reserved.

No part of this book may be reproduced, stored in a retrieval system, or transmitted by any means without the written permission of the author.

First published by AuthorHouse 3/5/2010

ISBN: 978-1-4490-3974-5 (sc)

This book is printed on acid-free paper.

DEDICATION

This book is dedicated to my wife Razia and my sons Nadeem, Zahir and Arif.

About the Author

Manzoor Moghal is a well-known writer and commentator in the UK and international news media and a lecturer on a range of subjects, including Uganda, Asians in Britain, race-relations, issues of global terror, the criminal justice system, Islam and Muslim affairs. He was born in Sialkot, Pakistan and grew up in Uganda where he had his early schooling. He returned to Pakistan to complete his education studying at the Foreman Christian College, Lahore, where he graduated with a degree in Sciences from Punjab University.

In Uganda he became renowned as an outstanding civic leader, a politician and a leader of the Asian community and had frequent dealings with the highest officials of the Ugandan administration, including Prime Ministers and Presidents. In his various capacities he contributed substantially to the social, community and political life of the country. He was forced to flee Uganda in September 1972 with his family and came to settle in Leicester.

Beginning life again in Leicester, he built a new business for his family whilst choosing initially to stay away from civic and political life, greatly disenchanted with the prevalent racism and attitudes he found in

Leicester and other British cities. In the early 1980s he began active involvement in public life. His most significant contribution was in the field of race-relations. As Chairman of the Leicestershire County Council's Race-Relations Committee, he and his colleagues changed the face of race-relations in the city and the county, and the period from 1984 to 1997 ushered in an era of harmonious race and community relations which over the years became the envy of the rest of the country. In 2001 he was awarded an M.B.E. in the Queen's Honours List. He is currently Chairman of the Muslim Forum, a think tank organisation.

Acknowledgements

I am very grateful to my son Arif for his enormous contribution in reading my manuscript and making corrections, and also for his valuable advice in the arrangement of the book. I am also grateful to my Assistant in my practice, Radhika Madhani, for her patience and diligence in arranging my manuscript and formatting other material for final submission to the publishers.

Introduction

Idi Amin was a uniquely fascinating character, always big news not only in Uganda and Britain but all the over the world. He made headlines everywhere, continually shocking and absorbing people with his words and actions and even more with the things he was said to do in private. He rose through his animal instincts and had no boundaries and no fears of repercussions for any act he deemed necessary or politic. I lived through those times and those upheavals in Uganda, and it was as he rose to power that I had first had contact and meetings with him and also those around him who fell in his wake. This is a unique insight and telling of his story from someone who heard and saw the physical smashing of his way to power both by tanks and shells and by the brutal murders of opponents in the streets of Kampala. In the end it was my own life that was in danger and I was lucky to escape alive with my family and come to England.

After I fled I continued to follow his fortunes closely. I always felt that Idi Amin had been seriously misjudged by the British, and he was lampooned by the media following the lead of the British government in order to camouflage their own shortcomings in their dealings with this man who had outwitted them at every turn. I first wrote this book largely for myself in the late 1970s as a memoir of my times in Uganda and a record of the facts I knew – facts that showed the cunning and guile of Amin and how he outmanoeuvred his opponents. Over the years I have read and heard much about Idi Amin. But I have seen no account that tells properly the stories of both the politics and the people involved, and at the same time places Amin's little-understood African intelligence at its heart.

I believe that what I have written will be of much interest to many readers, not only those who know about Idi Amin and Uganda but also those who may not have come across this subject at all.

Manzoor Moghal
Leicester, July 2009

Prologue

I fled Uganda with my wife and children in the middle of the night on 9th September 1972 to escape death. Just three days earlier I had learnt that I was named on a hit list of individuals who were to be exterminated. It was the most traumatic experience of my life, and right until our plane took off from Entebbe Airport I was in fear for our lives.

My wife and I had left Uganda on 19th June 1972 to attend the Lions International convention in Mexico City following my election as District Governor for Uganda, Kenya, Tanzania and Ethiopia. After the convention we made a tour of Canada, America and Europe and returned to Uganda on 30th July 1972.

We had hardly unpacked when I had to fly to Nairobi in Kenya with my father who needed some specialist medical treatment. It was there I heard Amin's announcement that the Asians were to be expelled from Uganda. My father and I immediately hurried back to Uganda.

For a few days I seriously thought of staying on alone in Uganda and sending my wife and three children away to Britain for their safety. However, based on the experiences of my recent visit and because one of my closest friends was already living there, I decided instead to go to Canada with my family. I traveled to Kampala to obtain the required documentation. But I did not even begin the process.

It was in Kampala that I learnt from a reliable source that I was on Amin's special hit list. Over the next two or three days I went into hiding and made further discreet enquiries. My life was indeed in danger. I could not wait to get permission to go to Canada. I and all the members of my family held British passports and I decided to flee to Britain as soon as possible. I immediately arranged to meet a top official at the British High Commission in Kampala to explain my position and seek entry into Britain without going through the process of 'validation' required to gain an entry permit, which would have taken several days. The official assured me that I would have no difficulty landing in London, especially as I had recently passed through on my return from Europe. I was told that if I was stopped at the airport in London I could refer the relevant officials to this meeting at the High Commission in Kampala.

Assured that I could gain entry into Britain, my plans gathered pace and I secretly made preparations to leave. Only my immediate family knew of my intentions. I had to be particularly careful as our neighbour was an army official.

On the evening of my departure I returned to my home in Masaka and destroyed and disposed of my private documents. My wife and I packed three suitcases with some clothes and we told our three young sons that we were going to Kampala. We included nothing that could betray our identification, hiding our passports in the car for use only when we arrived at the airport. We removed nothing from the house that might give away our intentions. All our keepsakes and family photos were left behind in the hope that they would somehow be sent on later. We did not even tell our loved and trusted maid, Mary, that we were leaving. She was left behind expecting to see us in two or three days.

Late in the evening my father drove us to Entebbe airport. We arrived at around 10pm and joined the heaving crowds and the simmering chaos and panic. There were no ticket sales offices at the airport. I placed my family in a fixed spot and went from counter to counter looking for any flight out of the country with spare seats. It seemed all flights to all destinations were fully subscribed, but when I reached the Lufthansa counter I found two seats to Frankfurt. I paid with cash and went to make a painful decision with my family. There were no named tickets - just two boarding passes.

My wife is a woman of immense strength and courage. During the days when I had gone into hiding in Kampala I had not been able to send her any word. She had waited calmly and with faith, telling me later of how she had stayed up in the nights listening to the sound of bullets without any doubt that I would return. At the airport she steadfastly refused to take one of the passes. There was no way I could physically force her through all the barriers and checkpoints and into a seat. I had broken cover and my life was in immediate danger. I knew she would not be persuaded - though I tried.

The time to the flight quickly passed. We had agreed I would take our eldest son and that she would follow with my youngest two. When we went to the Lufthansa counter for the final formalities my wife and I made our goodbyes in the restrained manner of our people and with true feeling towards our sons. One of the attendants at the counter witnessed our parting and told us to wait. She disappeared and returned some minutes later. She had realised that a family was about to be dangerously separated and had gone to see if anything could be done. She returned telling us that three more seats had been made available in the first-class section. She held up the flight for half an hour while she made the necessary arrangements.

At the customs desk my wife was made to give up all her jewellery.

Alone we crossed the tarmac and the darkness. A silver jumbo gleamed and waited for us in the night. Only when it left the ground did my mind rest.

We took a connecting flight from Frankfurt and arrived in Britain at Heathrow on the morning of September 10th with our three suitcases and £100. Everything else was lost. But we were together.

Chapter One

General Idi Amin Dada, self-appointed President of Uganda and ruthless military dictator, was overthrown from power in February 1979. After staying for just over a year in Libya as President Gadaffi's guest he went into exile in Jeddah in the Kingdom of Saudi Arabia under the protection of the Saudi royal family. For nearly nine years he had been the absolute ruler of a nation once so prosperous and beautiful it had been known as the 'Pearl of Africa'.

Today in the West he is seen as a brutal tyrant who ruled Uganda with an iron fist, striking terror into the hearts of his enemies; responsible for the deaths of hundreds of thousands of innocent Ugandans, a murderous barbarian, lampooned as a lunatic buffoon with syphilis of the brain; an illiterate, diabolic and ruthless dictator who would swat human lives with as little concern as he would swat a fly. He was even alleged to have eaten human flesh - apparently 'too salty' for his taste.

Though unquestionably ruthless, my own experience of Amin belies the rest of this image. He was certainly unpredictable, and therefore difficult to understand and deal with. But he was also an affable and shrewd man, and his public buffoonery would always translate into a more subtle charm in private or closed meetings that would beguile and seduce the unwary, and until his final military adventures he was also a proven strategist, as this account will show.

In his prime in Uganda Amin was a remarkably fit and agile person despite his great height and bulk. He was a giant of a man, well over six feet tall and weighing some eighteen stone. For several years whilst serving in the army he was Uganda's undisputed heavyweight boxing champion. His British officers thought of him as a splendid fellow, and he basked in their adulation.

It is true he was poorly educated, twice failing exams for military promotion, and that when he came into power he spoke broken and often incomprehensible English. But this was of no concern to him. Gradually, and to everybody's surprise, he became reasonably articulate and learnt to express himself clearly and forcefully in English. He was a man seemingly without fear and convinced that not only would he leave an indelible mark on Uganda but that he would also be remembered by the whole world for centuries to come. When he captured power in January 1971 he catapulted himself into the role of a great African hero and for a time millions of Africans would love and respect him for his courage and flamboyance at home and in the face of the West.

When he first came to power Amin was hailed as the man who liberated Uganda from the despotic and oppressive rule of President Milton Obote. Within a short space of time he became one of the best-known leaders in the whole of the world but because of his maverick behaviour he remained a puzzling phenomenon. His knack for survival was uncanny, and though luck could be said to have had played some part in elevating this hulk of a man to the dizzy heights of a leader whose name bestrode the continent, his success was mainly due the devastatingly effective use of the tools at his disposal combined with an uncommon ability to correctly anticipate the moves and even the thoughts of those who opposed him. To his mind anyone who opposed him in any way was his enemy. Once he detected even the slightest hint of any opposition from any quarter he acted with lethal swiftness, pouncing unexpectedly on his enemies and annihilating them. The methods he used were brutal and direct and, though far from unknown in mankind's long history, were certainly not the like of which were seen in the more developed countries of the West. But the West, and Britain in particular, made a grave error in ridiculing him and refusing to try and understand him because he seemed to them beyond the pale of civilisation.

Though he would never have used such a term, Amin was a practising Darwinist. His every instinct was based on the concept of the survival of the fittest. This was the simple key to understanding him which if grasped could have unlocked many problems. His military mind was trained, disciplined and completely attuned to this firm belief. To Amin the Ugandan people whom he came to rule were important, but the men of his army were closest to his heart. They were the ones who enabled his methods of natural selection. He made no secret of the fact that their welfare took precedence over everything else and that this was paramount in all his thinking and all his actions. He treated every challenge to his power, both real and perceived, as a battle in which he, as a military commander, had to vanquish the adversary swiftly. His key tactics were shock and surprise. In almost every confrontation with the West and all those who assumed themselves to be superior to him and his black compatriots, Amin nearly always emerged successful, not only in defeating them but also in having them humiliated in the process before delivering his coup de grace.

In all his moves there was always an underlying game plan that his more educated opponents did not grasp. Outwardly he appeared clumsy and even clownish, but this had the effect of putting his opponents off their guard. Far from this naive and buffoonish exterior his unlettered mind absorbed and analysed all that was around him.

Until his overthrow in 1979 he had chalked up an impressive record of successes against his enemies and withstood a number of attempts on his life. His rule took its toll on hundreds of thousands of human lives and shattered the economy of a once prosperous and highly respected African nation. But he survived it all.

Idi Amin was born into a Muslim family of the Adibu clan of the small Kakwa tribe in the West Nile District of Uganda bordering southern Sudan in the 1920s. (The Muslims of this area are generally referred to as Nubians.) His given names were Idi Awo-Ongo Angoo. His father was a Catholic named Adreas Nyabire who converted to Islam in 1910, taking the name Amin Dada. Amin Dada senior served in the 4th King's African Rifles (KAR) from 1915 to 1920 and joined the Uganda Police in 1921 where his job was to administer corporal punishments to the natives. His mother was called Assa Aatte. She was a highly respected woman and sought-after traditional herbalist renowned for dealing with pregnancy and fertility complications. Amin's parents were married in 1921 and Amin was to be the youngest of their three children. His elder brother and sister both died in the early 1930s. His parents separated in 1931, allegedly over suspicion as to whether Amin's genetic father was actually one Daudi Chwa. He grew up with his maternal family in Luwero and worked for a time as a goatherd when he was around ten.

In 1940 Amin went to live with a maternal uncle in Bombo and tried to register for formal schooling, but he was rejected because Nubians could not then get admission to schools. He is said to have taken part and been injured in the Nubian anti-discrimination riots in the same year. In 1941 he was accepted by the Garaya Islamic School in Bombo and attended until the end of 1944. At Gayara he showed that his was a mind of potential, excelling in and winning honours for his skills in Qur'anic recitation in 1943. After leaving he got a job as door attendant and hat and coat checker at the Imperial Hotel in Kampala. It was here that he impressed a British officer who recruited him into the army.

He joined the King's African Rifles, probably in 1946, though he himself claimed to have seen action in World War II in which he further claimed to have distinguished himself for bravery. One thing though is clear. As a soldier Amin was hardworking, diligent, daring and brave, and recognition of these qualities (over and above his failure in written exams) by his commanding British officers led to quick promotions.

Before Uganda's independence he was one of the only two Ugandan African NCOs (Non Commissioned Officers), both of whom were hastily promoted to full officer ranks just before Uganda attained its full independence on 9th October 1962. (It would have been extremely embarrassing for both Britain and Uganda if there had been no Ugandan African officers in the Uganda army at the time of independence.)

There is evidence that a few months prior to Uganda's independence Amin came under suspicion of having murdered some Turkana tribesmen in the Northwest part of Kenya bordering the Karamoja District of Uganda. The Kenyan authorities, then under British rule, wanted to take criminal proceedings against Amin. But Sir Walter Coutts, the last British colonial Governor of Uganda, persuaded them to return Amin to Uganda where he proposed to deal with the matter himself. After reviewing the case Sir Walter came to the conclusion that the minimum punishment for Amin for the incident should be his dismissal from the King's African Rifles. However, before announcing Amin's dismissal he thought it expedient to consult Milton Obote, who was then the Prime Minister in Uganda's self-governing authority prior to the country's full independence. Obote who did not then know Amin personally disagreed strongly with the course of action proposed by Sir Walter, and instead recommended that Idi Amin only be severely reprimanded for his misconduct. It is said that Sir Walter warned Milton Obote that Idi Amin would prove troublesome in the future. But Obote paid no heed and Amin emerged unscathed. Luck had been with him on this occasion.

In the late 1950's there were two principal political parties vying for power in Uganda; the Uganda People's Congress (UPC) and the Democratic Party (DP). The UPC was founded and led by the skilled and heavily left-leaning orator Milton Obote who came from the Langi tribe of northern Uganda. The DP was founded and led by the right-leaning western inclined Benedicto Kiwanuka of the Baganda tribe of central Uganda.

Obote's UPC drew great support from all areas of Uganda apart from the Kingdom of Buganda. It was a time when Uganda's politics revolved around the issue of independence, but despite Obote's excellent credentials in this area and notwithstanding his best efforts he could not create any significant support for his party in Buganda. This was crucial because whoever won control of Buganda was almost certainly guaranteed to win control of Uganda, because Buganda had by far the largest population and electorate of any province in Uganda. Theoretically, this should have left the way clear for the Muganda Kiwanuka. (People from Buganda are described as Baganda in the plural and Muganda in the singular. Hence, the Muganda Kiwanuka, from the Kingdom of Buganda can also be described as coming from the Baganda tribe.) Kiwanuka did in fact go on to win the general election of 1961. This election gave the country internal self-government and was meant to provide the government for post independence Uganda. Kiwanuka was elected Uganda's first Chief Minister and would soon style himself as the country's Prime Minister, but his victory would prove hollow and ultimately futile.

The 1961 general election had been boycotted by the vast majority of Baganda through their official political group the Kabaka Yekka (the Luganda for Kabaka Only) because of a severe disagreement over the issue of direct versus indirect elections in Buganda to choose the Baganda members of the new Ugandan Parliament. Buganda had a centuries old institution called the Lukiko, composed of unelected tribal chiefs and leaders which acted as a provincial parliament for the region. (In the 1961 election the Lukiko included for the first time some elected representatives.) The Lukiko had insisted that the 21 Baganda to be elected to the Uganda national Parliament must be decided upon by the result of an electoral college formed wholly exclusively from the Lukiko. Initially this idea had received no backing from either the DP or the UPC so the British had felt free to take little notice of the Lukiko and expected the planned boycott to have little impact. But in fact the boycott was almost complete. The Baganda are a fiercely loyal people and took full notice of the instructions of the Lukiko which acted on behalf of their beloved and respected hereditary leader, the Kabaka, the King of Buganda, Sir Edward Mutesa.

In the 1961 general election Kiwanuka's Democratic Party had won through in Buganda solely because the handful of Baganda who did come out to vote for him did so because they were Catholics, and the Catholic Kiwanuka was being heavily backed and endorsed by the Catholic Church. (In Masaka, for example, out of an electorate of between four and five thousand registered voters only three to four hundred cast votes.) But the majority of the Baganda were Anglicans, like the Kabaka himself, and took no notice of the Catholic Church's endorsement. The vociferous minority Muslim Baganda also demonstrated their loyalty to the Kabaka and fully backed the boycott. The British were forced to sit up and listen again to the demands of the Lukiko. They had good reason to because there were now some stirrings of unrest in Buganda which already had a history of vigorous campaigning against the British rule. In fact the main political agitation for Uganda's independence had its origins in Buganda, and for a long time the Baganda politicians were in the vanguard of the independence movement. Economically, culturally and politically the Baganda were and still remain the most advanced tribe in Uganda, and they have always been conscious and sometimes arrogantly assertive of their superior position in the country. They formed the backbone of Uganda's civil service, and geographically and politically were at the centre of all important activities in Uganda. (Kampala, the commercial capital of Uganda, is located in Buganda.). The Kabaka of Buganda was the most powerful of all the kings and tribal rulers in the country and all of them looked upon him, often with envy, as the dominant player in shaping the political destiny of the country.

Milton Obote had realised beyond a shadow of doubt that if he were ever to assume the leadership of an independent Uganda it was absolutely imperative for him to find some common ground with the Kabaka Yekka group of the Baganda by somehow gaining the blessing of the Kabaka. The wily Obote found his opportunity after the boycott of the 1961 general election. As well as making certain promises to the Kabaka, he gave his backing to the idea that the Lukiko should send forward Baganda representatives to the national parliament through an electoral college. Foolishly, Kiwanuka would not budge on the issue. But with the backing of the UPC the British felt able to organise fresh elections in 1962 with the system demanded by the Lukiko.

The new elections were a disaster for the Kiwanuka's Democratic Party. The Baganda remained vehemently opposed to Kiwanuka not only because he had opposed the demands for indirect elections in Buganda for representation in Uganda's Parliament, but because he had also affronted the dignity of their most beloved Kabaka with his arrogance. He had even openly boasted in public meetings of his superior political and governmental powers, thus adding fuel to the fire. This coming from a subject of the Kabaka (all Baganda are the subjects of the Kabaka) was reprehensible and totally unacceptable to the Buganda establishment. The UPC/Kabaka Yekka alliance duly overcame the Democratic Party in the 1962 elections and the Langi Obote became the first Prime Minister of an independent Uganda.

In order to secure Buganda support Obote had also made certain other concessions and promises to the Kabaka Yekka, including the promise to elevate the Kabaka to the office of the President of independent Uganda, and the allocation of some important ministerial portfolios to nominees of Kabaka Yekka. As a result of this the Kabaka became the first President of Uganda. In Obote's mind the non-Executive office of the President was and would remain purely symbolic and sinecure. The Kabaka, however, who had always exercised supreme power as the undisputed ruler of Buganda, thought and acted otherwise.

Following Obote's emergence as Prime Minister, real power in the country came to be vested increasingly in his hands and in his well organised party machine. His alliance partners, the Kabaka Yekka, felt uncomfortable with this shifting in the power base, and soon murmurings of dissatisfaction, dissent and broken pledges began to be heard. On the advice of his closest confidants and advisors the Kabaka began adopting an aggressive and sometimes belligerent attitude in the exercise of his powers. Obote, meanwhile, was further consolidating his power base. By offering very attractive inducements he was able to lure several Kabaka Yekka members of Parliament who represented Buganda into the ranks of his Uganda Peoples Congress. In a short period of time most of the Kabaka Yekka members of Parliament had defected to Obote's UPC. From the opposition benches several members of the Democratic Party also crossed the floor for similar considerations further swelling ranks of the UPC. This one-way traffic of defections from the opposition benches to the government side left the opposition terribly emasculated. Obote's power became supreme power and as time went on he was increasingly able to ignore the Kabaka and impose his own will.

The once powerful Kabaka Yekka was in total disarray. Obote now felt more than confident in bullying the Kabaka, especially on the issue of the "Lost Counties". These were counties which had once been part of the neighbouring kingdom of Bunyoro until 1894 when they were annexed to the kingdom of Buganda by military force. The Banyoro still disputed Buganda's authority over these counties, and for years had demanded their return. When the British departed from Uganda on 9th October 1962 they left this thorny problem unresolved, although certain provisions had been made in Uganda's new constitution for dealing with this matter at a later time. In striking an accord with the Kabaka before the 1962 elections, Obote is believed to have given definite assurances to the Kabaka that despite the provisions of the Constitution, which clearly required the holding of a referendum in the disputed counties within a period of two years of Uganda's independence, he would somehow ensure that the counties would remain part of Buganda. But when Obote had fully consolidated his hold on power and no longer needed the Kabaka Yekka as his allies he reneged on this unwritten promise. In accordance with the constitutional requirements he was able to declare the holding of a referendum in the disputed counties.

The Kabaka, obviously angered and offended, was faced with a situation where the interests of his Kingdom clashed with the obligations of his Presidential duties. Understandably he chose to side with the interests of his kingdom and, therefore, refused to sign the instruments of referendum when they were sent to him by the Parliament.

But for Obote this was a minor technicality easily resolved by getting Parliament to authorise him as Prime Minister to sign instead.

Just before the referendum in 1964, secure in his own political strength and clearly tired with the intransigent attitude of the Kabaka and his followers on the Bunyoro counties issue, Obote officially terminated the shaky alliance of his Uganda Peoples Congress with the Kabaka

Yekka group. The handful of Kabaka Yekka members of Parliament who had steadfastly refused all temptations to defect to the UPC left the government benches and joined the thinning ranks of the opposition.

Despite growing threats of rebellion from the supporters of the Kabaka the referendum was held on schedule. The vote was overwhelmingly in favour of rejoining Bunyoro. It had been a forgone conclusion because the majority of the voters were Banyuro. Nevertheless, it was a terrible and humiliating blow for the Kabaka and from this point onwards the tension between the Kabaka and Obote increased steadily and without respite. The Kabaka sensed an impending confrontation and began to make certain tentative moves to safeguard himself. His advisors and supporters assured him daily of the undying loyalty of the Baganda people to their Kabaka, and the Kabaka took further reassurance in the fact that Uganda's Chief of Staff, Brigadier Shabani Opoloto, was also a friend of his and loyal to him. This particular connection with Opoloto was immensely valued and it was believed that in the event of any confrontation with the Prime Minister the President's position would remain secure as a result.

Chapter Two

Idi Amin had a very special charm which when mixed with an ebullient joviality and a unique charisma could sometimes, remarkably, combine to produce almost the innocence of a child. These qualities enabled him to win the confidence of his associates, disarm his opponents and camouflage his real intentions. He conveniently hid behind this façade and thereby outwitted many more educated and powerful politicians. It was in this way that he was able to win the confidence of Milton Obote who would eventually elevate him to the highest position in Uganda's Armed Forces, the Commander-in-Chief and Chief of Defence. Within a short time Obote came to rely on him as a loyal and trustworthy ally.

In 1965 Idi Amin, by then the Deputy Commander of Uganda's Army, faced another serious threat to his position and survival.

The famous "Gold and Ivory" case came to light in September 1965. The reverberations from this episode almost toppled Milton Obote from power in February 1966. The Congolese nationalists who were fighting President Moishe Tshombe in the neighbouring Congo Republic (later named Zaire, and now renamed the Congo) were buying arms for their struggle through

Uganda, and to finance the purchase of the military hardware they had smuggled large quantities of money, gold and ivory into Uganda from the Congo. It is believed that Obote, who was openly sympathetic with the cause of the Congolese nationalists, had authorized Amin to make all the necessary arrangements for assisting the Congolese in buying their requirements.

In a sensational revelation in September 1965 Daudi Ocheng, a northern Member of Parliament, who was also a very close friend and supporter of the Kabaka, disclosed details of large and unaccountable sums of money which had found their way into Idi Amin's bank account. Ocheng had somehow come into possession of a copy of Amin's bank statement which showed this information. As a result Amin was suspected of having converted to his own advantage the larger portion of gold and ivory brought into Uganda by the Congolese nationalists. It was openly alleged that this was done in connivance with Milton Obote and some of his closet cabinet ministers, all of whom were said to have had a share in this embezzlement. Despite the furore Uganda's Minister of Defence, Felix Onama, dismissed the allegations as untrue and promised Parliament that the matter would be investigated thoroughly. Gradually after this palliative promise the uproar quelled.

The government seemed to have limited the damage and controlled the situation. But in February 1966 while Milton Obote and some of his Ministers were touring the country, a motion tabled by Daudi Ocheng proposing Idi Amin's dismissal as Deputy Commander of the Army for his complicity in the embezzlement of the Congolese money was passed by Uganda's Parliament with only one dissenting vote. This act was a direct and open challenge to Milton Obote's power and it shook the nation. But Obote could be a shrewd politician and reacted calmly to this grave and threatening situation. On his return to Kampala he held an emergency meeting of his cabinet and in his address to them he asked all those cabinet ministers who agreed with Parliament's resolution for the dismissal of Idi Amin to resign from the government. No Minister resigned. A few days later, in a dramatic and ruthless move, five cabinet ministers whom Obote was convinced had conspired to usurp power from him were arrested in a cabinet meeting over which he was presiding. The next day Idi Amin was promoted to Army Chief of Staff, replacing Brigadier Shabani Opoloto who was moved sideways to the position of Chief of Defence Staff. This effectively took away Opoloto's hold over Uganda's Armed Forces. Amin's loyalty to Obote was amply rewarded, and Brigadier Shabani Opoloto, who was suspected of pro-Kabaka sentiments, was shunted away. Opoloto was later dismissed from office and then interred.

Later a Judicial Commission, headed by a Judge of the East African High Court and assisted by Judges of the Kenya and Tanzania High Courts, found no evidence to substantiate Daudi Ocheng's allegations against Milton Obote, Idi Amin and the others alleged to have taken part in the embezzlement. They were all officially exonerated by the findings of this Commission. Throughout the episode of the Congolese gold and ivory scandal Amin's position had been very precarious, and had it not been for Obote's confidence in him he may well have faced an ignominious end.

With Opoloto out of the picture and Amin in place as Army Chief of Staff Obote now felt able to dismiss the Kabaka as President of Uganda in April 1966 with impunity. The Kabaka in turn seemed to enter into a strange frame of mind. Either because of being ill advised or because of a stubborn belief in his own unassailability, he failed to gauge the political and physical dangers he was being exposed to by Obote's machinations. Having been arbitrarily dismissed as President against his wishes he refused to move out of the Presidential Lodge at Makindye, near Kampala, and was reported to be moving around the grounds of the Lodge armed with pistols, fully confident that any intruders could be repelled. The Kabaka for a time was in such a belligerent mood that no one could bring home to him the reality of what had transpired and the great danger to which he was personally exposed. But to the relief of many a confrontation was avoided when he later left the Presidential Lodge of his own accord and moved to his Palace on Mengo Hill. However, this would prove to be merely a respite.

In the meantime the Buganda Lukiko had accused Milton Obote and his Uganda People's Congress of having illegally abrogated the 1962 Constitution of Uganda, and passed a resolution ordering Milton Obote's central government (located in Entebbe) and Uganda's Parliament (located in Kampala), both on Buganda territory, to get out from the Kingdom of Buganda. Obote was infuriated and knew that it had now become imperative for him to act quickly and resolutely to end this dispute.

Despite the obviously untenable stance that his Lukiko had taken the Kabaka would not climb down.

He was badly advised by those who had his ear. He felt confident of his strength, and believed that if Obote resorted to force to bring him down his small band of bodyguards and the Buganda Police backed by a massive civilian uprising would overwhelm Obote's forces. The dye was cast for a life and death confrontation between the Kabaka and Milton Obote.

The Armed Forces of Uganda were then predominantly made up of the northern tribes: the Langi (Obote's own tribesmen) and their neighbours the Acholi. The command of the army was now in the hands of General Idi Amin who was then loyal to Obote. Thus Obote was able to count with confidence on the loyalty of the Armed Forces. Assured of his strength he sent Amin with a small band of soldiers to the Kabaka's Palace on Mengo Hill with orders to search the Palace grounds for arms which reportedly were being stockpiled in preparation for an armed conflict with the central government, and to arrest the Kabaka if he met resistance. Amin was instructed by Obote to use minimal force in carrying out this very difficult and delicate task.

When Amin tried to enter the palace grounds he encountered stiff resistance and a shoot out erupted between his soldiers and the Kabaka's policemen. Amin's first attack on the palace was repelled. In his second attack he deployed a much larger and better-equipped force. The fighting was very heavy, and as the day wore on it became clear that the Kabaka could not be over powered as easily as had been anticipated. I was told by some of his close associates that the Kabaka himself was engaged in the fighting, and was believed to have machine-gunned several of Amin's soldiers. The casualties were heavy on both sides, and when Amin realised that it was going to be difficult to capture the Kabaka he ordered his tanks and planes into action.

On that fateful day in May of 1966 I had travelled the 82 miles from my hometown of Masaka to Kampala to attend a meeting of Uganda's Urban Authorities Association of which I was the Vice-Chairman. Our meeting at Kampala's City Hall was to be attended by representative Councillors and Town Clerks of all the urban local authorities in Uganda. It was scheduled to start at 10 am and I had arrived half an hour early. As the delegates started arriving we were told of roadblocks mounted by the army at some of the entry points into Kampala. The Chairman of the Association (the Mayor of Mengo Municipal Council) failed to turn up, so as Vice Chairman I presided over the meeting and in view of the reports of unrest brought it to an early close. As we dispersed we heard the news of Amin's attack on the Kabaka's palace, and as I drove around on the main streets of the city shortly afterwards I saw a number of army Land Rovers moving at great speed loaded with the bodies of dead and wounded soldiers, some hanging out from the back of the vehicles.

Amin's tanks were bombarding the palace walls relentlessly and I could see his planes dropping flame bombs on the palace buildings. As most of the buildings within the palace grounds had thatched roofs they were soon ablaze and I could see the rising flames and plumes of smoke. In the midst of this mayhem the cornered Kabaka secretly fled with some of his most trusted bodyguards. His men had put up great resistance but in the face of overwhelming firepower and numbers they were eventually overrun by the government forces. This was a great victory for Idi Amin and his soldiers.

The Baganda realised that the battle had been lost and there was great anxiety in their minds regarding the safety of their king. But he had made it to safety. That very afternoon I received a secret message from a journalist friend of mine confirming that the Kabaka had secretly left the palace for a safe hide-out, and was perhaps on his way out of the country. I was relieved and pleased that the Kabaka was safely away.

Most of the telephone lines to Kampala were cut, and I spent the next three days with a friend in Kampala unable to get any news to my family in Masaka. These were worrying and anxious times. But eventually, on the fourth day I was able to travel to my home in Masaka with an army convoy. Except for our convoy there was absolutely no other traffic on the 82-mile stretch that we travelled. The road seemed to have been dug up partially at one place along the way, but there were none of the obstacles or roadblocks which the army had expected and I reached home safely.

In the aftermath of the Mengo Hill battle Amin's soldiers took cruel revenge on the Baganda captured inside and outside of the palace grounds. There were some rumblings of an uprising against Milton Obote in some parts of Buganda, and indeed some Police Stations were attacked by loyalist Baganda. But these were isolated incidents and the government forces were quickly able to crush all the rebel elements.

The Kabaka had been a thorn in Obote's flesh. Obote had removed the thorn and humbled the proud Baganda, and was now the undisputed master of the country.

Chapter Three

Obote now began to shape Uganda in his own image. He projected himself as a truly progressive socialist leader, endowed with great intellectual ability. His move to the left was symbolised by the famous document he issued called the "Common Man's Charter", characteristic of his higher aspirations both for himself and Uganda. With the radical proposals contained in this charter he wanted to embark upon a unique political experiment in Uganda designed to galvanise the masses into a party oriented political movement, who would then transform Uganda into a powerful and prosperous socialist state transcending tribal loyalties. At the same time he hoped to dilute the army's rule in the political life of the country. The armed forces had kept him in power, but he was not unaware of the dangers posed by relying too heavily upon them. Unfortunately for Obote, subsequent events made the role of the armed forces even more significant in Ugandan politics.

Following an assassination attempt on Obote's life in December 1969 the army cracked down brutally on the civilian population of Uganda, especially the Baganda. This new wave of terror against the Baganda brought new and even more intense feelings of hatred towards Obote and his regime. It also exposed his Achilles heel: his dependency on the army to keep him in power. Despite his best efforts with the Common Man's Charter, his civilian base of support was to remain seriously eroded. Obote had made himself unpopular even amongst the non-Baganda people of Uganda when he pensioned off their kings and tribal rulers. These high handed and arbitrary actions were made possible through a new constitution that Obote drew up by which he became the President of Uganda with full executive powers.

Brigadier Pierino Okoya was the second in command of Uganda's army. He was intensely loyal to Milton Obote and it was widely believed that he was being groomed for higher office. Idi Amin's growing power in the armed forces and his cockiness had begun to disturb Obote. Okoya seemed a very suitable candidate for replacing Idi Amin at an appropriate time, and in pursuance of this objective Obote began bestowing favours on Okoya. Brigadier Okoya played his part and evinced great public concern for Obote's safety after the assassination attempt, and he publicly accused Idi Amin of cowardice for reportedly running away into hiding on hearing of the attempt on Obote's life. Clearly Okoya's confidence and influence were growing. Amin's alert mind was quick to grasp that the implications of these developments posed a very serious threat to his position.

A few days after Okoya's criticism of Amin, both Okoya and his wife were found dead outside their village home. They had been murdered. This was shocking news for Obote, but apart from expressing his horror and sympathies he said nothing regarding the circumstances of the deaths. Amin made no comment at all and was conspicuously absent from the funerals of the dead Brigadier and his wife, although as Commander of the army he would have been expected to attend the funeral of a senior army officer. His absence was commented upon in many circles, and the rumour mill ground out only one theory.

Initial evidence gathered by the Criminal Investigation Department (CID) of Uganda on the Okoyas deaths indicated that the murders were committed with guns similar to those in use by the Uganda Army. Because of the circumstances preceding the Okoya murders doubts began to be cast in Amin's direction and it was argued that he was the person who stood to gain most from Okoya's departure. Obote's plans had been derailed and he was determined to find the perpetrators of this crime. On his instructions the CID of Uganda, headed by the zealous, efficient and widely dreaded Asian police officer Mohamed Hassan, set into motion a full-scale investigation and Amin was subjected to an intense interrogation. (The results of this interrogation never came to light, and in fact none of the evidence amassed by the Police was ever disclosed, but it is widely believed that it placed Amin under very strong suspicion of direct involvement in the killings.[1*]) Amin was aware of the

---

[1*] On Amin's capture of power Hassan's safety was in obvious jeopardy and he was advised by close friends to flee Uganda immediately. One friend even offered him the use of a private jet so that he and his family could slip out of Uganda unnoticed from a northern location far from Entebbe and Kampala. But Hassan prevaricated. He had only just recently made a substantial investment in a block of flats on Kololo Hill in Kampala and he was unwilling to abandon it. Moreover, his senior colleague in the police force Erianayo Oryema, the Inspector General of the Police, had somehow managed to quickly rehabilitate himself with Amin and had in fact been promoted to a ministerial post in the Cabinet. Hassan foolishly thought

gathering storm around him. But during this turbulent period he continued to perform his normal duties whilst quietly assessing and strengthening his support in the armed forces.

By the end of 1970 Obote had a new thorn in his flesh – Amin. He desperately wanted to be rid of him. He could have suspended him and then dismissed him or dismissed him outright, but he was not sure how the army would react to such a move so he had to move with extreme caution. He was aware of the strong loyalty Amin commanded, especially in the lower ranks of the army, and he did not want to risk a rift which could result in his own downfall. To achieve his objective Obote embarked on a carefully planned strategy of systematically whittling down Amin's power and influence by discrediting him in the eyes of the army and the general public. He tried to deflate Amin's ego and cut him down to size by deliberately ignoring him on several public and private occasions. Quite often, and with increasing frequency, Amin had to cool his heels outside Obote's office when

---

that with his colleague's help he too might be spared any retribution. He was arrested a few weeks later and thrown into Uganda's notorious Luzira prison. Friends and relatives who were allowed to see him brought back appalling stories of the conditions under which he was being held. They reported that he was regularly beaten by the prison guards and given very meagre rations. His appearance was shocking. As time went by his morale was completely broken and he would cry and beg his visitors to do something to help him. He was then moved on to a prison close to the southern border with Tanzania where he was allowed very few visitors and held under even worse conditions. Whoever saw him spoke of a brutalised skeletal figure constantly wishing and begging for the release of death. Hassan died here when he was shot by guards who alleged that he was trying to escape. His body was brought to Kampala under armed guard and quietly buried two or three miles from his flats in Kololo. Those who prepared the body for its final rights described a single shot to the head, seemingly at point blank range.

he went to meet him. On one occasion Amin got trapped into appearing on Uganda's state television with a panel of highly educated civilians and military officers from his army to discuss issues relating to Uganda's armed forces. The show was an unmitigated disaster for him. Amin's inability to understand some of the questions put to him in English was embarrassingly evident, and as the show progressed it appeared that the whole exercise had been engineered to humiliate him and make him look like an idiot who was undeserving of the position that he had come to occupy in the army. But Amin was not a helpless fool, and despite his handicap with the English language and his consequent embarrassment he remained quite cool and alert. To cope with the difficult situation he deployed a sure fire tactic. Whenever he failed to understand a question, even after it was repeated, he resorted to praising Milton Obote's wise leadership and pledging his undying loyalty to him. Whatever the question he laughed off his shortcomings and continued to heap praise on President Milton Obote. This novel approach completely disarrayed his would be tormentors.

A few days later I met up with some Sandhurst trained officers that I knew. They privately laughed at the farcical performance of their commanding officer, but they would never dare to speak deprecatingly of him in public; such was Amin's hold on the armed forces even at that time when he was being systematically humiliated by Obote. To protect his position and mollify Obote, Amin made repeated statements, both in private and in public, saying that he would never allow a military coup in Uganda because Milton Obote was such a great and wise leader, and he would always remain loyal to him. But Obote was too clever to be swayed by such platitudes. He had already made up his mind to dump Amin and moved him sideways to the position of Chief of Defence Staff. The implications of this 'promotion' were too well known to Idi Amin, as this was the position to which his predecessor, Brigadier Shabani Opoloto, was shunted before being dismissed in disgrace and then later imprisoned.

Suddenly Amin's normal movements seemed to have come under some restriction and he became noticeably less visible. He was scarcely seen in public, and his unexplained absence from various official functions which he normally would have attended was commented upon. His children who were usually driven to their school every morning in an official chauffeur-driven Mercedes Benz suddenly stopped attending school giving rise to rumours in Kampala that Idi Amin had been placed under some kind of house arrest by Milton Obote. But Amin remained unruffled by these developments, and it seemed that despite some tentative moves to remove him the President was unable to act decisively for fear of an uprising by troops loyal to Amin. As mysteriously as he had disappeared from the public eye he resurfaced in some style by making an appearance at a special ceremony at Makerere University in Kampala where Obote was being installed as the University Chancellor. Though Amin was not accorded the VIP treatment commensurate with his position, and despite being jeered by some students, he mingled jovially with the crowd, and appeared to pay little attention to his apparent demotion in the social hierarchy.

Amin was a courageous person, especially when it was a question of self-preservation, and he consciously timed his actions to achieve the maximum impact. Even when the investigation into the Okoya murders was being vigorously conducted by the CID chief, Mohammed Hassan, and Amin was in serious danger of being implicated in the crime, he continued to maintain a cool exterior.

In a direct challenge to Milton Obote he gave the people of Uganda a further taste of his daring behaviour at a huge Muslim "mauledi" (celebrations marking the birth of Prophet Muhammad) held at Bwala Hill in my hometown of Masaka in August 1970. Addressing this large gathering he held a copy of the Qur'an in his right hand and declared loudly and clearly that he was afraid of no one but Allah. This mammoth gathering of Muslims was presided over by Prince Badru Kakungulu, uncle of the late Kabaka of Buganda (Kabaka Edward Mutesa had died while in exile in London) and the leader of the Muslims in Uganda. The tone of Idi Amin's defiant declaration, the context in which it was made and the venue where it was delivered amounted to a direct challenge to Obote, who at that time was considered a threat not only to Amin but also to Prince Badru Kakungulu's leadership of Uganda's Muslim community. His defiant speech, considered by some as foolhardy, was tumultuously received by the huge crowd of his fellow Muslims who cheered him all the more for addressing them fluently in their own language. The Baganda take great pride in their language and culture and simply love the non-Muganda who speaks their language well. The crowd loved him and showed no restraint in their adulation of the man.

By his mere presence among the Kakungulu group and by his defiant declaration of fearing no one but God he had identified himself with Prince Badru and followers and all the Baganda who had been continually battered by Obote and his government. He was also in his way publicly atoning for the sin he had committed when he had attacked the Kabaka in May 1966.

Also at that time the Baganda Muslims had a new reason for hating Obote. On top of dethroning their Kabaka, he had divided the Ugandan Muslim community by promoting his cousin and fellow Langi Muslim, Adoko Nekyon, as a national Muslim leader.

With Obote's blessing and encouragement Nekyon had launched a new national Muslim organisation called the National Association for the Advancement of Muslims (NAAM). He was the head of this new organization and under its banner he created a new structure of Imams (Muslim clerics who led the congregations in prayer) in Uganda. Nekyon placed his own appointees as Imams to most of the mosques in the country and chose the Grand Mufti (chief cleric) to be at their head. This new national Muslim organisation was recognised by Obote's government as the official representative body of the Muslims in Uganda. But despite this official government recognition and encouragement, and despite vigorous efforts by Nekyon and his close supporters to popularise their organisation, they could not make any significant inroads in Buganda and their success in the rest of the country was also patchy. In Buganda the vast majority of Muslims remained solidly behind the leadership of Prince Badru Kakungulu, and he continued to enjoy some support in the rest of the country as well.

The large and imposing mosque in Masaka, which had been built largely with funds from the Asian Muslim community and with generous contributions from the spiritual leader of the Khoja Ismailia community, Prince Karim Aga Khan, was taken over by Nekyon in duplicitous circumstances, and an Imam from his group was installed there to lead the prayers, thereby effectively taking over the mosque. As Nekyon's Imams were officially recognised by the government, and as they were given full police protection whenever needed, the Kakungulu group, in order to avoid confrontation with Nekyon, moved out en masse from this mosque quietly and held their Friday congregational prayers and all their other activities at the Bwala Muslim School which was some two miles away. With this mounting pressure from Nekyon's NAAM group and the unfriendly if not positively hostile attitude of the Obote government, followers of the Kakungulu group felt increasingly intimidated and isolated. As a consequence they were praying almost daily for deliverance from Obote's oppression and misrule.

Against this background Amin's association with the Kakungulu camp and his daring challenge to Obote gave new hope to these beleaguered Muslims. They had quite unexpectedly found a new champion in the powerful figure of Idi Amin. He was instantly acclaimed as a great Muslim leader and fervent prayers were said for his well being.

Later, after he had seized power Amin made a special journey to Bwala Hill to commemorate the historic event of his fearless challenge to Milton Obote. At an elaborate and well publicised ceremony organised by the Muslims of Masaka Idi Amin laid the foundation stone of a new mosque which the grateful Muslims of the District proposed to build on the very spot from where he had delivered his fearless challenge to Obote as a permanent commemoration of the event. As a Muslim leader I was involved in making the arrangements for this occasion and assisted Amin in the foundation stone laying ceremony. We had met formally two or three times before and we exchanged friendly pleasantries, expressing our hopes for Uganda's future.

The mammoth gathering at Bwala Hill on that day demonstrated a solid sense of unity amongst the Muslims of the area, who not very long ago had been badly divided by the machinations of Adoko Nekyon. It seemed as if the Muslims had buried their differences overnight and were behaving as if they had never known any serious internal differences. Even high church dignitaries, including the Bishop of the Diocese of Masaka, Bishop Adrian Ddungu, had joined the Muslims in celebrating Idi Amin's victory over Milton Obote with such a degree of enthusiasm that this new found unity of purpose between the Muslims and Christians seemed a little unreal. I knew the Bishop well and we exchanged views. He was a very pleasant, cultured and articulate person, and it was always a delight to talk to him and listen to his words of wisdom. Prince Badru also quietly confided to me as a friend that he was somewhat awed by the occasion. Both the Bishop and the Prince marvelled at the unbelievable transformation that had suddenly taken place in the attitude and behaviour of the people of Uganda who had found a common purpose in such a short space of time. In the expression of his private thoughts to me Prince Badru seemed to be saying that he felt the whole affair was somewhat surreal. Prince

Badru felt that the inter-denominational and inter-religious harmony that was being demonstrated may have been orchestrated to please the new regime. But in my opinion the upsurge of unity amongst the people of Uganda was generated by genuine sentiments of affection and loyalty to Idi Amin who had got rid of the demon Obote; it had little to do with the fear and terror that were later to become the mainstay of his power base. The crowd really loved Amin that day, and when he spoke to them in their Baganda language their ecstasy knew no bounds. They lionised him like a great conquering hero. Their adulation of him reminded me of the outpourings of Baganda sentiment on the triumphant return from exile of their beloved Kabaka, the late Edward Mutesa in 1955. Amin had truly become the hero of the Baganda people. Throughout the event they continued to show their love for him in an unabashed manner. They did not tire of heaping praise and gifts of cows, goats, fowls and farming land on him. Amin revelled unashamedly in this atmosphere of unprecedented and lavish hero worship, and in return would show his gratitude to the Baganda in many ways. In his government cabinet he surrounded himself with many Baganda Ministers, and later he took a Muganda bride whom he claimed had been given to him by the people of Buganda in appreciation of his services to the nation!

Chapter Four

Obote had committed to attending the Commonwealth Heads of Government meeting in Singapore in January 1971. Despite the problems he was having with Amin he flew to Singapore confident in the ability of his close colleagues to deal with any situation that might arise in his absence. In fact, he was so confident of his strength that before his departure he upbraided Idi Amin and his Defence Minister Felix Onama for some serious financial discrepancies that had come to light in the Auditor General's report, and had demanded a written explanation from them to be submitted to him on his return from Singapore. Over £2 million of army money had disappeared, and large quantities of guns had been found missing from the military armoury. Following this Amin knew beyond any doubt that a showdown between him and Obote was imminent: he knew that once again he was on sticky ground and his survival was in jeopardy. But Obote's absence from the country gave Amin his opportunity.

On 25th January 1971 he struck in a lighting move pre-empting the plan by Obote to have him arrested on charges of murdering Brigadier Okoya and his wife. Officers and troops loyal to Obote put up some resistance, but they were ruthlessly put down by Amin's soldiers. At the time of the coup d'etat Obote commanded great loyalty amongst the educated elite of the armed forces and he had almost total support from the Langi and Acholi soldiers who formed the bulk of the army. Amin's support came mainly from a small band of fiercely loyal Nubian soldiers and several uneducated junior officers for whom Idi Amin was a great role model. Various estimates indicate that at the time of the coup the troops loyal to Obote substantially outnumbered those loyal to Amin, and therefore Obote's men should have been able to overpower Amin and his supporters with relative ease. But Amin and his small band won the day: the speed and surprise of his strike combined with an utter ruthlessness in dealing with the enemy were the keys to his victory. Obote's men were caught unaware, virtually with their pants down, and quickly succumbed to the ferocity of Amin's attack. (The soldiers and officers who helped Amin in toppling Obote would later be hugely rewarded by Amin in many different ways. Many became rich beyond their wildest dreams.)

Before his overthrow Milton Obote had been looked upon by some African politicians as the new rising star in the firmament of African politics. He had seemed a politician of great sagacity endowed with a deep understanding of African politics. Although his countenance seldom ever conveyed any warmth or friendliness, his oratory was impressive and incisive. Following the downfall of Kwame Nkrumah, the charismatic leader of Ghana who had relentlessly and vigorously fought for African freedom from the thralldom of decadent western colonialism, it seemed as if Obote had taken over his mantle as Africa's champion. Obote had become a strong and vociferous critic of apartheid in South Africa, and condemned Britain in the strongest terms for its failure to deal effectively with the Unilateral Declaration of Independence (UDI) in Rhodesia in 1966 (renamed as Zimbabwe post independence.) He had openly threatened to leave the Commonwealth if Britain under the Tory government of Edward Heath resumed sales of arms to South Africa. This issue had aroused considerable controversy at the time, and the countries selling arms to South Africa had been viewed as supporters of apartheid. In this stand he was strongly supported by Tanzania under the leadership of President Julius Nyerere and Zambia's President Kenneth Kaunda, both of whom had also similarly threatened to quit the Commonwealth. In fact, Obote's main reason for going to Singapore was to present his case to the Conference and spell out to Britain and the other Commonwealth countries the implications of Britain's intransigent attitude on the issue of arms sales to South Africa. At the conference in a biting invective Obote unleashed a scathing attack on Britain's policies on South Africa and Rhodesia, and he went on to expose systematically the hypocrisy of Britain's platitudinous statements and its total lack of any constructive action against Rhodesia to remove the illegal regime of Ian Smith. The British reeled under the unexpected ferocity of the barrage of criticism, and despite some efforts by Edward Heath, the British Prime Minister, to calm the situation the British found themselves floundering and exposed in the total nakedness of their deceit and double standards.

It was most humiliating for Britain to be thus exposed, particularly by the leader of a small African country that not very long ago had been an insignificant part in the backyard of its mighty Empire. Obote revelled in the glory of his own performance in the cause of African freedom. But unfortunately for him, this was to be his last star performance. As he prepared to return home in triumph he was deposed by Idi Amin's coup. On hearing of this on his way back he stopped in Nairobi to assess his position but dared not return to Uganda for fear of losing his life at the hands of Amin and his soldiers. He fled to Tanzania where he bided his time under the protection of his friend and comrade President Julius Nyerere.

On hearing news of Obote's downfall Britain breathed an ill-concealed sigh of relief. The British had become increasingly uncomfortable with Obote's brand of politics. It was widely believed that Britain's well organised intelligence network in Uganda had had advance knowledge of Amin's moves in preparation for the coup, and therefore, had they wanted to, they could have conveyed this information to Obote well in time to enable him to quash Amin's plot. This was confirmed by British government documents declassified around the year 2001 under the thirty-year rule. They clearly indicated that Amin's rise to power was orchestrated to some degree by outside interests particularly opposed to Obote's nationalisation and Africanisation drives, in which the state had taken a 51 per cent share in all foreign and Ugandan-Asian owned industries. Uganda was a vital source of raw materials to the west and Obote was on the verge of changing the whole political system in Uganda at the expense of the non-black entrenched interests.

Plans had already been laid by the British in concert with the Israelis and Americans to stop Obote in his tracks, and Obote finally and thoroughly cooked his own goose with his virulent attack against British policies on South Africa and Rhodesia. Britain was deeply offended and no moves were made to protect Obote. Just days before the coup 700 British troops arrived in neighbouring Kenya, ostensibly to help quell any anti-British rioting in response to Heath's decision to sell arms to South Africa. They were not deployed in any capacity and Obote was deposed.

In the later years of his rule Milton Obote's administration had declined alarmingly. This was due to the favouritism, nepotism and corruption that had steadily crept into most of the government departments of his once efficient administration. Often, unqualified and thoroughly incompetent people were appointed to top positions in many public and governmental organisations. The following is one example.

The post of Chairman of Uganda Planning Board was an important appointment to an important body that was responsible for all land planning matters in the urban areas of the country. Uganda's misfortune in this case was one Dr Akiki Nyabongo, qualified by relation to the former ruler of one of the defunct kingdoms of Uganda. He always took pride in associating himself with the common people of Uganda, maligning them grossly by equating them with his own shabby attire and behaviour. He was an old man, perhaps even a little senile. The origins of his 'doctorate' were obscure. He claimed to have obtained the qualification from an unknown American University. He had scant knowledge of land planning matters, and he took little interest in the subject. Whenever he visited any local authority he was more interested in what that authority had to offer him by way of alcoholic drinks than in discussing any of their planning matters. He often arrived at the Masaka Municipal Council without informing anyone, and upon arrival insisted on being served with whisky, his favourite libation, and provision of other alcoholic drinks for his shabby entourage, irrespective of the time of the day. (One or two hangers-on who were totally unconnected with any local authority business usually accompanied him.) On these occasions, after thoroughly availing himself of the free supply of drinks provided by his embarrassed hosts, he would chatter on incoherently and endlessly about related and unrelated local planning matters of which he himself understood very little. He could seldom hold any sensible discussion on any one topic for any length of time, and often rambled on in a monologue about unrelated matters. I was then the Chairman of the Planning and Development Committee and the Deputy Mayor of the Masaka Municipal Council. My fellow Councillors, senior officers of the authority and I had to sit and listen to this man's nonsense simply because he held a position given to him by the dreaded Milton Obote. During some of these sessions he often gave vent to his baser sentiments of anti-Asian racism, and indulged in unabashed self-praise of his own accomplishments in the United States and in Uganda. Although he spoke very ungrammatical English with a pseudo-American accent, he prided himself on his self-proclaimed faultless English. He was almost always uncouth, shabbily dressed and was accompanied by equally shabby looking hangers-on who expected equal hospitality. He was a joke. Unfortunately for those concerned – a bad joke.

The whole western world gave Idi Amin a rapturous welcome to the international community when he overthrew the hated regime of President Milton Obote. They all acclaimed him as a saviour of Uganda who had freed Uganda from the corrupt, repressive, dictatorial and pseudo-socialist regime of Obote. Britain was the first country to recognise Amin's military regime with almost unseemly haste within just two or three days of the coup, and the British press was not far behind in hailing Idi Amin as Uganda's new hope and wishing him good fortune.

The first overseas visit that Idi Amin made was to Britain in 1971 at the invitation of the British government who entertained him lavishly, much to his pleasure. He lunched with the Queen at Buckingham Palace, and was flown to his cherished Scotland in a special plane provided by the government where he indulged in his love of the Scottish bagpipes. (Amin had trained in a Scottish military band while stationed at Fort Hall in Kenya in 1950.)

The British government and the British press were favourably impressed by Idi Amin's performance and talked of a new era of co-operation and understanding between the two countries. The British government could not hide its pleasure at the departure of the insufferably arrogant and clever Milton Obote and his replacement by the uneducated and often clumsy Idi Amin, whom they assumed would be easily malleable in their hands.

Idi Amin's lack of education and his total inexperience of government were considered as assets by the British government and they felt confident that they could mould him to suit their purposes. Amin's several pro-British pronouncements were very encouraging to Britain, and were considered propitious signs for British interests in Uganda. Little did they then realise that their diplomacy would suffer unprecedented body blows from the brutal force of this man's cunning mind. However, at that time his visit was an unmitigated success, and Amin returned home in great spirits, buoyed by the generous aid that he had been offered for Uganda.

Milton Obote's overthrow had been greeted with particular jubilation in Buganda where resentment against him was very deep. The Baganda never forgave him for forcing the Kabaka into exile in England where he had suddenly and somewhat mysteriously died, and for dismantling their ancient kingdom of Buganda and with it destroying their traditional institutions of government. In London the Kabaka, who as a king was used to a very lavish lifestyle, had been forced to live in the docklands area in virtual penury with no choice but to live on the handouts of the social security system and the charity of some of his well-wishers. The circumstances of the Kabaka's sudden death gave rise to suspicions amongst the Baganda that somehow the wily Milton Obote had engineered the premature demise of their king, who was a threat to Obote's power as long as he lived. The Kabaka's autopsy report stated alcohol poisoning as the cause of death, but despite this the Baganda remained sceptical and unconvinced. It was a well-known fact that the Kabaka was used to heavy and even excessive drinking, and it was not easily believed that with his very limited financial resources he would have been able to indulge in the extravagance of the massive drinking bout that would have been needed to kill him. Moreover, rumours that a beautiful Langi tribeswoman had been sent by Obote to London to beguile the Kabaka added fuel to these misgivings. These theories left a strong suspicion in the minds of many Baganda that the Kabaka's sudden death was the result of some diabolical plotting by Obote. Hence, if there was not already reason enough, when Obote was deposed from power by Idi Amin none were happier than the people of Buganda who showed their joy by ecstatic dancing in spontaneously organised mammoth street demonstrations. For the Baganda, Idi Amin was indeed their great liberator.

To take advantage of the favourable political climate in Buganda and to further cement his own position, one of Idi Amin's early moves was to bring back to Uganda the body of the Kabaka from its temporary place of burial in London and give it a most befitting royal burial in the traditional ways of royal burials in Buganda. This was an act of great political sagacity and shrewdness, and also an indication of Amin's then sincere desire to restore the Baganda to their rightful place in the country. When the Kabaka's body arrived back in Uganda, his subjects were able to see the body of their king which had been preserved and encased in a glass casket. Thousands of the poor, weeping Baganda thought that their king was merely sleeping and that he would rise up in a dramatic fashion to rule his country once again. In a blaze of publicity and in a series of very impressive ceremonies the Kabaka's body was laid to rest in the royal burial grounds at Kasubi in Buganda. The Baganda were extremely grateful to Idi Amin and hailed him as a great humanitarian. In the euphoria of their new status in Uganda, the Baganda began to hope that the kingdom of Buganda with a Kabaka as its ruler would be restored under the benign and wise leadership of President Idi Amin. The Kabaka's eldest son Prince Ronald Mutebi, who was then schooling in England and who had accompanied the body of his late father to Uganda, was Amin's honoured guest. Despite his youthful years Prince Mutebi behaved impeccably during his father's burial ceremonies and was given a lot of prominence throughout this period. Because of this the Baganda soon started talking openly about putting him on the vacant throne of Buganda as their next rightful king. Many Baganda elders and chiefs went to see Idi Amin about this issue, and he listened to them with great interest and patience. He allowed these Baganda to discuss this matter freely with Prince Ronald Mutebi himself. He even allowed the convening of a Baganda Elders Conference which was to discuss this issue comprehensively and make suitable recommendations to Amin. He had genuinely wanted to please the Baganda, but he had hoped that in view of the seemingly insurmountable difficulties in mounting the exercise of restoring the Kabakaship the Baganda elders would decide against such a move, at least in the short term. However, when he saw that the current was going in the opposite direction he quickly quashed the whole notion of bringing back the monarchy. He told the elders of the tribe that he had done them and the people of Baganda a great favour by restoring to them the body of their king and giving it an official burial with full honours, and that they would have to be content with what he had already done for them. He wanted to hear no more talk about the restoration of the Kabaka. This blunt rejection by Amin dampened the enthusiasm of the Baganda, but Amin's military rule made it impossible for them to pursue this matter any further. They were clearly disappointed in Amin but despite this snub they still considered him to be a lesser evil than the hated Obote, and therefore continued to cooperate with his regime.

Amin's other popular move on coming to power had been to order the release of all the political detainees who had been incarcerated on Obote's orders. Those released came from all walks of life in Uganda. They included the five former cabinet Ministers of Obote who had been arrested so dramatically, and the leader of the opposition Democratic Party, Benedicto Kiwanuka, who had been imprisoned in 1969.

After a long period in the wilderness, during which he had watched helplessly the total destruction of his once powerful Democratic Party and the desertion of his closest political allies who had unashamedly rushed to join the swelling ranks of the mighty Uganda People's Congress of Obote, Kiwanuka longed to re-emerge with some strength on the political scene of his beloved country.

To consolidate his position Amin gave some of the released detainees important positions in government and foreign embassies. In this atmosphere Kiwanuka soon came to the forefront again as Amin's chief spokesman in Buganda and was soon after to be elevated to the position of Chief Justice of Uganda's High Court – the position of his final downfall.

Kiwanuka was no self-seeker. In his own right he had been a highly successful barrister, and enjoyed considerable affluence. He had felt deeply honoured in accepting the appointment as Chief Justice, particularly as he was the first black Ugandan-African to hold this high office. He was in no way motivated by the financial rewards of office and all along he genuinely had Uganda's interests at heart. I had known him personally for many years, and we had met and talked in public and private meetings from the time before Uganda's independence right until a few months before his death when he had been the guest of honour at a charity evening I had organised in Masaka.

In private I had always found him to be a capable and intelligent person. But in more public arenas he was prone to displaying an almost naïve political immaturity. When Kiwanuko became Uganda's Chief Minister in 1961 he failed to realise the extent to which his following had been eroded in Buganda by the Baganda boycott of the 1961 general elections, and that he had further alienated himself from the Baganda masses by his presumptuous and arrogant attitude towards the Kabaka. The Baganda were not tolerant of any one, least of all one of their own, insulting the Kabaka. When he became Chief Minister, some of his well wishers suggested to him that he should seek an audience with the Kabaka in order to repair some of the great damage that had been done to the relations between his Democratic Party and the followers of the Kabaka. Instead of giving serious thought to this wise suggestion he turned it down point blank, and said very bluntly and publicly that he had no need for such a meeting and that if Kabaka wished to see him, then the Kabaka should have to travel to Entebbe (seat of Uganda's central government) to meet him. He contended that he as the Chief Minister of Uganda could not stoop to seek an audience with the hereditary ruler of a small part of the country. I was present at an open-air rally in Masaka that Kiwanuka addressed, and I could not believe my ears when I heard him assuming this stance in a public meeting. I had known him for some five years by then and could not have imagined how he had become so deluded. It seemed power had gone to his head. If Kiwanuka had been a more seasoned and astute politician he would have leaned over backwards to keep some of his options open with his fellow Baganda politicians. Even though he was Chief Minister, as a Muganda he still remained a subject of the Kabaka. If he had shown some respect for his king by requesting a meeting with him, and by going over to see him, he would have endeared himself enormously to the people of Buganda and he would have changed the fate of hundreds of thousands.

The results of the 1962 independence general elections gave no clear majority to either Obote's UPC or Kiwanuka's DP, but crucially Obote received the full support of the whole block of Kabaka Yekka members of Parliament because he had astutely backed the Kabaka's demand for indirect elections in Buganda for its representatives to the Uganda Parliament, whereas Kiwanuka had insisted that there should be direct elections. As a result Kiwanuka's DP suffered a most humiliating defeat in Buganda in the elections to the Buganda Lukiko (Buganda's Provincial Parliament), which was to act as an electoral college to choose the 21 representatives of Buganda to Uganda's Parliament. When the time came to choose, the Lukiko with its 21 MPs installed Obote, a Langi tribesman from the north, in power. If Kiwanuka had kept some of his options open with the Kabaka, he could have negotiated an alliance of some sort with his fellow Baganda. But for Kiwanuka's foolishness the history of Uganda would have been totally different.

The Catholic Church of Uganda that had been largely responsible for the earlier political successes of Kiwanuka was also sadly instrumental in his downfall in the 1962 general elections. They believed that despite the vigorous campaign mounted by the Kabaka Yekka in the 1962 general elections, the Catholics of Buganda would give their solid backing to their protégé, Benedicto Kiwanuka. It was because of this miscalculation and complacency that Kiwanuka's Democratic Party floundered in Buganda. The Catholic Church failed to judge the depth of the loyalty of the Baganda to their Kabaka - loyalty which transcended all other considerations. When the Baganda people were told by Kabaka Yekka that the Democratic Party threatened the institutions of their kingdom and the position of their king, the vast majority of Baganda of all faiths - Protestants, Catholics and Muslims - rallied behind their king. What the Catholic Church and Kiwanuka did not realise was that the allegiance of the Baganda to the institution of Kabakaship and their ancient way of life was deeper and stronger than the roots of the white man's religion to which they had been converted not so very long ago.

In later years when he was in the political wilderness he realised the enormity of his folly and tried desperately to ingratiate himself with the Kabaka. He made several attempts to get the Kabaka's blessing to be nominated as a Member of Parliament from the Buganda Lukiko, but the Kabaka never forgave him, and he failed in all his efforts to make a comeback. Kiwanuka's political career was effectively ended, until his brief but tragic reappearance in the Amin administration.

After his elevation to Chief Justice, Kiwanuko showed his gratitude to Amin by lavishing him with praise wherever he went. The Baganda, some of whom had earlier shunned him for his anti-Kabaka posturing, liked this new set-up and started looking upon him as a possible successor to Amin if and when Amin decided to hand over power to a civilian government as he had promised. On seizing power Amin had not immediately assumed the title of President, but chose instead to be styled as the Military Head of State. This lead to the belief in many quarters, especially among the Baganda, that Amin's military regime was of a temporary nature and they hoped that he would soon fulfil his promise of an early return to civilian government. But these hopes were soon dashed when Amin chose to be known as the President of Uganda.

In a calculated move Amin chose not to abolish the Constitution of Uganda but tailored it to his needs by issuing various decrees. The Constitution of Uganda provided that in the event of the President's incapacity or his death, the Chief Justice of Uganda was to assume full Presidential powers, pending a general election to be organised within a specified period of time. Benedicto Kiwanuka and his supporters were not unaware of this provision in the Constitution, and naively encouraged the wide dissemination of this information. The Baganda liked what they heard, especially since it was enshrined in the country's constitution. It was reassuring for them to know that in the event of anything unfortunate happening to Idi Amin the leadership of the country would fall into the hands of their fellow tribesman. Instead of keeping this discreet they began to trumpet it around the country. Kiwanuka himself took pleasure from discussing this situation within his own circle and foolishly even brought the matter up in some public rallies. Obviously Amin, being well informed of all political matters in Uganda, did not like what he heard about the publicly expressed hope of the Baganda. He promptly put paid to the premature hopes of the Baganda by issuing a decree repealing the relevant clause in the constitution.

As part of his consolidation strategy, and to acquire more respectability in the country, Amin took Kiwanuka with him on most of his tours in the country, particularly in Buganda where Kiwanuka had a renewed following. On one such tour to the town of Masaka, a strong-hold of the Catholics, in the course of introducing Amin to a mammoth gathering on the golf course, Kiwanuka complimented Amin on the great love which the people of Masaka District had shown for him by showering him with gifts of hundreds of cows and goats (with thousand of fowls thrown in) and large tracts of good farming land in appreciation of his valour in overthrowing the hated regime of Milton Obote. He said, perhaps jokingly, that when Amin retired from his onerous duties as President (presumably after fulfilling his promise to restore civilian rule in the country) he would be kept profitably occupied in looking after the huge flocks of animals and the hundreds of acres of land given to him by his loving fellow-citizens. These light-hearted remarks of Kiwanuka in talking about Amin's retirement were ill conceived, because Amin never had any thoughts of retiring from his position of supreme power. Amin did not fail to notice the great enthusiasm with which the crowd that was predominantly Baganda received Kiwanuka's remarks about his possible retirement from the Presidency. I was present during these proceedings, and having heard what Kiwanuka had said so unwisely I came to the conclusion that he had inadvertently jeopardized his own life. The incident also revealed, rather glaringly, Kiwanuka's own ambition to come into power from a civilian base, hopefully reinforced by Amin's armed forces. Since Kiwanuka harboured even the thought of replacing Amin at some future date, this in Amin's eyes made Kiwanuka an enemy who posed a threat to his power. Amin lost no time in placing Kiwanuka under the closest surveillance of his Secret Service.

A few months later Kiwanuka compounded his naivety when he granted an application of habeas corpus filed by the British High Commissioner in Kampala for a white Briton named Donald Steward who had been detained by Amin's soldiers. On granting the application he severely criticised the manner in which Steward had been unlawfully detained. The content and the tone of his ruling was a severe indictment of the high-handed methods of Amin's regime. Kiwanuka's poor judgement had kept him in the political wilderness long after Uganda's independence. Now it was to seal his fate. There was no pressing reason for him to issue his judgement in such a strong manner. To be fair he was an upright man of sincere beliefs, conditioned perhaps by his strong Catholic background, but in pillorying Amin's regime which by implication meant Idi Amin himself, Kiwanuka had effectively signed his own death warrant. Maybe he wanted to tell the whole western world that despite Amin's high-handed methods and despite the atrocities of his regime, in him Uganda still had a strong, wise and western oriented voice, prepared to chastise some of these un-Christian practices. Whatever the reasons, Kiwanuka had grossly misjudged Amin who would never tolerate such pontificating from anyone, least of all from one whom he had himself appointed. He had been a marked man for some time and after this ruling many politicians feared for his safety. Subsequent events proved that their fears were well founded. But Amin wisely did not rush the issue. In order not to create an immediate confrontation with his Chief Justice and precipitate a crisis, Donald Steward was deported to Britain on Amin's direct order immediately after the court ruling with the minimum fuss.

A few days later Kiwanuka's life was ended. He was dragged away from his High Court chambers by some Africans, alleged to be members of Amin's Secret Service, and never heard of again. There were rumours that he had been brutally murdered on the same day, and his body then chemically dissolved. In any case, no trace of his body was ever found. Poor Kiwanuka died defending the rights of a foreigner, a white British subject whose worst fate without his intervention would have been a few more days or weeks of detention in Uganda's prison, where, according to his own account he was treated very well, and provided with food from one of the best hotels

IDI AMIN: LION OF AFRICA

in Kampala. It is extremely unlikely that the British government would not have successfully intervened on Steward's behalf had the need arisen. Kiwanuka did not have to pay for Steward's early liberty with his own life.

The Catholics in particular and the people of Uganda in general lost a highly respected God-fearing politician and sincere leader.

Francis Walugembe, unlike Benedicto Kiwanuka, was a wily and adept politician. It was Francis to whom I first voiced my fears for Kiwanuka after his court ruling on Donald Stewart. We had sat in my office on the day of the judgement and shared our disbelief over the day's events. Francis would never have made such an obvious error. Yet he too was to fall victim to Amin's ruthless vigilance and suspicion of any potential enemies. His death was to be a particularly cruel and tragic example of Amin's methods.

Francis Walugembe was a constantly significant and influential figure in the Ugandan political scene. A charismatic Muganda politician who had occupied senior powerful ministerial positions in the Buganda kingdom, he was a well-educated, intelligent and articulate person. He had been a Minister in the Kabaka's government and on several occasions acted as Buganda's Katikiro (Chief Minister). At the time of Amin's coup he was Mayor of the municipality of Masaka.

Walugembe had cleverly managed to keep afloat on the Ugandan political scene after Amin came into power. Whilst many of Obote's supporters had been liquidated by the Amin regime, or had retired from active politics to save their necks, after a brief and adroit period in hiding

Walugembe was making efforts to wriggle back into the corridors of power and regain a position for himself in the country. He was in close contact with Uganda's Foreign Minister Wanume Kibedi and some other influential cabinet Ministers who were close to Amin. They intimated to him that he was being seriously considered for a cabinet post. Whether or not Walugembe was to be offered a cabinet post, there were strong indications that he was going to be given an important political role in the administration of the country. He had had a number of meetings with Amin, encouraging Amin to judge him from close quarters. It was in one of these meetings that Amin himself gave Walugembe confirmation of a forthcoming appointment.

When Amin announced the re-organisation of the Ugandan provinces with new provincial names and redrawn boundaries he also announced that new Governors would be appointed to these newly created provinces. Walugembe was promised the province of Ankole/Buddu. His appointment to the post of Provincial Governor was a near certainty, and an announcement to this effect was eagerly awaited by him and by his friends, myself included. But it seems Amin may have been merely stringing Walugembe along, keeping him in close view while it suited his purposes. Amin never entirely trusted Obote's former followers, especially those who were well educated, and he may have suspected Walugembe of actively harbouring pro-Obote sentiments. Walugembe, rather than winning Amin's confidence, had been under the constant surveillance of the Secret Service.

Walugembe was well aware of what was happening in the country under Amin's rule and was not happy with many of the developments. On more than one occasion he had given vent to his sentiments in private conversations with me and some of his other close friends. I had known Francis for several years, and had worked very closely with him on several political and social issues. He was also a family friend. He was appalled at some of the injustices of the Amin regime and had no love for military dictatorships of any kind. He certainly knew of some of the killings that had taken place. However, he was a realist and always bent with the wind when the occasion demanded. It was this ability of his that had kept him afloat in the choppy political waters of Uganda. He was confident that by maintaining some measure of loyalty to Amin and by becoming part of his administration for as long as it was expedient he would be able to survive successfully until, hopefully, the climate changed for the better. But sadly he was being betrayed by some one close to him, and the noose of Amin's Secret Service was tightening.

Once Amin got confirmation of his suspicions, he ordered his top hatchet man and favourite murderer Major Malyamungu to deal with Walugembe. Malyamungu, based at the Masaka Army Barracks, had a great inward contempt for the suave, smartly dressed, handsome and articulate Walugembe and received the instructions to kill him with sheer delight. He proceeded to carry out his orders in such a brutal fashion that even Amin must have been shocked by the sheer barbarity which Malyamungu and his men used in finishing off Walugembe.

Only a few days before his death he telephoned me one evening saying that he wanted to see me urgently. We arranged to meet in my office. We talked about the prevailing political scene in the country and we exchanged our fears and anxieties for the well being of the country under Amin's oppressive rule. He openly voiced fears about his own life and told me in no uncertain terms that the lives of all educated and influential people in the country were at risk. He realised that he was walking a tightrope and that any slip might cost his life. He spoke of going again into hiding. If he had wanted to he could have easily fled Uganda, but his confidence in his own ability to survive and his close contact with Amin was reassuring him for the time being. He suggested with great emphasis that I should at least adopt a low profile and hide myself for my safety if I could not quickly arrange my own exit from Uganda. He did not for one moment doubt his own ability to over-ride all the difficulties in some way. He miscalculated, tragically.

After a long and public chase through the streets of Masaka, Francis was cornered by Malyamungu and his soldiers. Even then he pleaded with his captors to contact Amin, whom he assured them repeatedly would tell them to spare his life. But his desperate pleas fell on deaf ears, and his captors proceeded to extract the last breaths of his life in a barbarous and heinous fashion. His was a death of a thousand cuts. Taking pleasure in their work his killers cut his body repeatedly; sparing him no indignity they cut away whole pieces of his hands, limbs and body gradually. He was tortured to a slow and excruciating death.

This gruesome event took place a few days after I had fled Uganda in the darkness of the night with my wife and children. When Francis had come to see me he warned me of the dangers lurking around me from Idi Amin and his hatchet men. I had already made up my mind to leave the country. Two weeks before my meeting with Francis I had been warned by a close friend that I was on Amin's hit list. After making some discreet inquiries and after discussing the matter with my late father I came to the conclusion that I had to leave Uganda with my family as soon as possible.

I was in Britain when I received the sad news of Francis Walugembe's brutal murder. I was later told how several Baganda, including some taxi-drivers, had taken part in chasing Walugembe through the streets of Masaka and were mainly responsible for his capture, and how they had stood by and watched the gruesome murder. Instead of being revolted by those acts of brutality they applauded the soldiers like cheerleaders. Some Baganda had hated Walugembe because he had switched his loyalties to Milton Obote after the overthrow of the Kabaka. Strangely and quite illogically many uneducated Baganda believed stories that Francis Walugembe had switched off the electric power which operated the Kabaka's automatic machine gun with which he had been supposedly mowing down Amin's soldiers in the upheaval of May 1966. They blamed him for the defeat of their Kabaka and now that supposed debt was paid.

Razia Moghal, Francis Walugembe, Mrs Walugembe and Manzoor Moghal, circa 1969

*President Idi Amin laying foundation stone
of new mosque at Bwala Hill, Masaka*

*Manzoor Moghal, Kabaka of Buganda Sir Edward
Mutesa, and Dr S B Kyewalyanga, circa 1964*

Francis Walugembe, Manzoor Moghal, Kabaka of Buganda Sir Edward Mutesa, circa 1963

Francis Walugembe, Kabaka of Uganda Sir Edward Mutesa, Dr S B Kyewalyanga and Manzoor Moghal, circa 1964

*Manzoor Moghal assisting President Idi Amin
at ceremony of laying foundation stone of
new mosque at Bwala Hill, Masaka*

President Idi Amin, Prince Badru Kakungulu and Manzoor Moghal, circa 1970

Benedicto Kiwanuka and Manzoor Moghal

Chapter Five

The Israelis had started an economic and political penetration of black Africa in the early sixties and had made considerable gains on both fronts within a few years. They had made many influential friends in these countries, and through them succeeded in blunting the force of the anti-Zionist propaganda mounted against them by the Arab world. They were increasingly seen as friends of the 'under-developed' countries and were openly welcomed by them. In Uganda the Israelis had arrived at the invitation of Milton Obote, and had become actively involved in training Uganda's armed forces, building roads, schools and industries, training technicians and a host of other activities. In a short time the Israelis became ubiquitous in all the important sectors of Uganda's life, and were a force to be reckoned with. Amin himself had done some training with the Israelis and initially had a great deal of time for them. (Later when he became President, he bought an Executive jet from Israel piloted by an Israeli for his personal use.) Even before his coup Amin had worked in close collaboration with the Israelis by allowing them to extend active military support to the southern Sudanese guerrilla group, the Anyanya, who were fighting for cessation from the Arab north.

Therefore, there was no reason why these friendly and mutually beneficial relations should not have continued after the take over by Amin. In fact, the relations were to be further strengthened, and Israel made promises of large-scale aid to Uganda to help Amin create greater prosperity in Uganda, and expand Uganda's Armed Forces.

Amin went to Israel at the invitation of its government and was greatly pleased with the warm reception he received there. Their promise of substantial aid to Uganda in particular was music to his ears. Amin expected the larger part of this promised assistance in the form of hard cash and sophisticated military equipment, but the Israelis argued that the aid they had in mind was to take the form of specific projects like buildings, industries, hospitals, roads, technical advice and some military equipment. The Israeli reluctance to give any cash, and meet his demands for sophisticated military equipment, which he reportedly wanted for mounting an invasion on neighbouring Tanzania to secure an independent sea outlet for Uganda, infuriated Amin and he felt betrayed. To meet his need for cash he started looking elsewhere, particularly in the direction of the Arab countries. He travelled to the Middle East and struck an accord with the charismatic Libyan leader, Muhammar Gaddafi, then an Arab leader of significant stature made fabulously rich from the oil revenues of his sparsely populated desert country. The Libyan leader, an implacable enemy of the Israelis and an avowed champion of all revolutionary movements throughout the world, promised massive aid to Uganda in exchange for Amin's promise to boot the

Israelis out of Uganda, and align Uganda firmly with the Arab world and the anti-Zionist movement. Amin, a Muslim himself, was quick to grasp this opportunity, and foresaw a long and beneficial relationship with the rich Arab countries. On his return to Uganda, he took the Israelis by complete surprise. He publicly expressed his solidarity with the Arab cause of Palestine and ordered all the Israelis out of Uganda, at the same time breaking off diplomatic relations with Israel. In his dramatic expulsion order he gave the Israelis very little time to organise themselves for an orderly departure. But the evacuation of the few hundred Israelis who worked in Uganda did not pose any major problem for the Israeli government. Those Israelis who could not fly from Entebbe to Israel were able to cross over into neighbouring Kenya by road, rail and air, for their onward journey to Israel from Nairobi. The Kenyan government maintained very friendly relations with Israel, and extended considerable assistance to the expelled Israelis. All remaining Israeli property in Uganda was officially confiscated by Amin. But he in fact gained very little from this act as the Israelis had managed to move most of their heavy equipment vehicles and personal belongings by road to Kenya.

The departure of the Israelis ushered in a new era of co-operation between Uganda and the Arab countries. Amin adopted a totally pro-Arab stance, and in repeated statements he heaped condemnation on the Zionists for usurping the Palestinian lands. The Arabs were absolutely delighted with Amin's performance. Not only had they succeeded in getting Israelis kicked out of Uganda, but in President Amin they had also gained an ally who was bold and vociferous in expressing his anti-Zionist sentiments. Moreover, the change in Israel's fortunes in Uganda was the beginning of the demise of their influence in black Africa. It was a remarkably successful piece of diplomacy by the Arabs. Amin too was delighted with his own performance, and was more than satisfied with the massive cash aid he began receiving from Libya and some of the other rich Arab countries. He believed that in the Arabs he had befriended powerful fellow Muslims allies on whom he could always rely for support and he had good cause to congratulate himself on his successful manoeuvrings.

The expulsion of the Israelis hardly provoked any retaliation or any serious repercussions from the outside world. It was an ill omen for the economically powerful Asian community of Uganda. These Ugandan Asians numbered some 60,000 at the time of Uganda's independence in October 1962 and were drawn from India, Pakistan and Bangladesh. In their history of settlement in Uganda, stretching back over a century, the Asians who had originally come as indentured Indian labourers to work on the railway line from Mombassa in Kenya to the hinterland in Uganda, had grown substantially in numbers, attracting enterprising shopkeepers, skilled workers, doctors, lawyers and engineers as well as more unskilled but eager labour from the Indian subcontinent. Most of these Indians (later to be called Asians because of the fragmentation of the Indian sub-continent, first into India and Pakistan, and later into India, Pakistan and Bangladesh) living in Uganda at the time of Uganda's independence were born in Uganda, and the others, mostly the older generation, had lived in Uganda for decades. They were an industrious and enterprising community, and as a result of their vigorous participation in the economic life of the country Uganda came to have a very healthy economy. The development of the various urban areas and a good road network in the country was largely due to the Asians, who had built practically all the towns and most of the villages in the country. Economically the Asians provided invaluable service, both to the indigenous people of the country and its colonial rulers. The British could not have ruled Uganda effectively without the services provided by the Asians, and Uganda's economy would have been considerably poorer without their participation.

The Asians were the first to teach the Africans the art of commercial trade and imparted to them various skills, turning many into skilled artisans. Sadly, during their colonial rule, the British did very little to further the Africans in the avenues of commerce and industry. They concentrated mainly on producing a class of petty African clerks to act as junior civil service administrators. The majority of the Africans seemed content to live in rural areas and remain working in the agricultural sector, growing the cash crops of coffee and cotton which were the country's main wealth. The Asian population on the other hand, for economic and social reasons, became mainly concentrated in the urban areas. Because of their preponderant numbers in all the towns in the country, their apparent wealth and because they looked and behaved differently from the Africans, the Asians increasingly became targets of criticism for the African politicians. They accused them of exploiting unfairly and dominating Uganda's economy and deliberately resisting integration with the black people of the country. In the twilight of their rule in Uganda, the British authorities belatedly embarked upon some crash business training programmes for the Ugandan Africans to teach them about commerce, but the results were disappointing. Instead of accepting blame for the failure of these grandiose programmes, hurriedly assembled as a showpiece to mollify African demands and complaints, the British experts and their African colleagues found easy scapegoats in the Asians. It was alleged that they were the stumbling blocks in the advancement of the black Africans in the field of business because they deliberately discriminated against them in their business practices. In fact one British expatriate business expert in the post independence era, a failed publican from England, publicly blamed the Asians for impeding the progress of the Africans, and strongly recommended the removal, forcibly if need be, of these Asians from the soil of Uganda to enable the black Africans to succeed in business. (His public statement was prominently reported by a leading national English daily newspaper.) The Asians were cast in the role of unscrupulous exploiters and villains who had amassed vast fortunes at the cost of the black people of the country, smuggling large sums of money out of Uganda, and depositing them in their fattening overseas accounts. The visible fact that the Asians owned most of the properties in the towns and often drove expensive cars further aggravated the situation. Of course, no regard was ever taken of the thousands of Asians who did not own properties and could not afford any sort of car at all.

Whilst it was true that Asians controlled a large part of the retail trade in Uganda and were involved in significant numbers in the import-export trade, wholesale distributions of goods, processing of Uganda's cash crops and several industrial enterprises, it is often forgotten that a small number of multi-national companies controlled from Britain and several other Europeans firms, some based in Kenya, controlled the cream of Uganda's trade. These establishments transferred their profits from Uganda to their foreign accounts on a massive scale, leaving the Asians way behind.

At the time of Uganda's independence in 1962, with the exception of a few hundred Asians who held Indian or Pakistani Passports, almost all the Asians were British subjects. The 1962 Constitution of Uganda gave certain rights to the Asians to acquire Ugandan citizenship within a prescribed time limit of two years, and conferred automatic citizenship of Uganda on those born of at least one Ugandan-born parent. The processing of applications for acquiring the citizenship of Uganda was left in the hands of Ugandan officials of the newly independent Uganda. Many Asians successfully applied for Ugandan citizenship immediately after independence. But several thousands who were unable to make up their minds quickly because of the uncertainties associated with the newly independent African states waited until the deadline and then applied in their thousands, literally flooding the Uganda immigration department with an avalanche of paperwork. This last minute rush caused long delays in the processing of applications. Hundreds of these applications went through the pipeline within a few months, but thousands (estimated to be between 12,000 and 15,000) remained unprocessed. When Milton Obote changed Uganda's Constitution, first in 1966 and then in 1967, the constitutional rights granted to the Asians in regard to their national status in the 1962 Uganda Constitution were effectively abrogated. The government without any consultation with the Asian community, and in violation of their rights, imposed an embargo on the granting of any more Uganda citizenship documents to the Asians whose applications had not been processed.

The state of gloom and despondency growing amongst the Asian community because of the political, business and social changes in the country under Obote deepened with this new development which clearly affected their survival in the country. The situation was aggravated even further as the government imposed restrictions on the trading activities of non-citizens. Under new rules approved by Obote's government non-Ugandan citizen Asians were increasingly denied trading licences in most rural and some urban areas, thus taking away their livelihood.

The Asians had good reason for delaying their decisions on citizenship applications after October 1962. Most harboured strong doubts about the ability of the black Africans to run Uganda's affairs peacefully, and feared an imminent eruption of violence mainly directed at their community. These sentiments were not without foundation. The 1958 Trade Boycott mounted by influential African politicians, and widely supported in the country against Asian traders, had frightened the Asian community. In this campaign African politicians deliberately inflamed anti-Asian sentiments amongst the populace and did irreparable damage to African-Asian relations. Asian shops in many parts of the country were burnt down. Many Asians were robbed and some were brutally murdered by gangs of Africans, ostensibly preaching the boycott of Asians traders. Asian owned businesses were bankrupted because of the intimidation which kept their African customers away. If the British authorities had not taken resolute steps to contain the situation this campaign of racial hatred would have escalated and taken an even greater toll of Asian lives and property.

The fears of the Asian community were further reinforced by the events in the neighbouring Belgian Congo in its immediate post-independence period in 1960. Thousands of Belgians were brutalized, robbed and murdered, and many of their women were raped in the barbaric orgies of violence indulged in by the Congolese army who appeared to have gone berserk. In the wake of these upheavals the Belgians fled the country, abandoning all their possessions. These fleeing Belgian refugees passed through Uganda telling harrowing tales of their experiences. Most of them had lived in Congo for decades, innocent of the crimes of the Belgian colonial authorities against the Congolese. Through sheer hard work they had built prosperous lives in the business, agricultural and industrial sectors of the country. But they had abandoned all hopes of salvaging any of their wealth, and considered themselves lucky to have escaped with their lives. For the Asians the fate of the fleeing Belgians provided tangible evidence of the possible scale of the black man's inhumanity towards his non-black neighbours.

At no time had the British put any pressure or used any effective persuasion to convince the Asian community of the desirability of becoming citizens of Uganda. On the contrary, the British left behind a lingering impression in the minds of the Asians that in any crisis which threatened their lives and property the British government would provide immediate protection for those Asians who had chosen to remain British subjects. The consequent false sense of security meant that many Asians clung on to their British passports as prized possessions.

Only when it became clear to the British Asians that their economic survival would be seriously jeopardized if they did not acquire Uganda citizenship did most of them apply for Uganda citizenship in the final stages before the deadline. (Of course, there were many Asians who never applied at all, having decided that they would either leave the country of their own volition or would go when they were forced to go. Some of these Asians left Uganda peacefully with all their possessions, in the early sixties, and settled in Britain, India, Pakistan, and Canada.)

Another important reason why the Asians clung to their British passports was that once they renounced their British nationality they were not allowed to regain it as a matter of right, and acquiring Ugandan citizenship required the total renunciation of British nationality. On the other hand, the white British subjects who became citizens of African countries had the right to revert automatically to their original British nationality as and when they chose to do so. Had some such provision been available to cover the British Asians as well large numbers of them would have unhesitatingly acquired Ugandan citizenship. Such an arrangement would have enormously benefited all parties; Asians, British and Ugandans. But on this vital issue of their national status, the Ugandan Asians were left in a hole by the British.

Since practically all the Asians in Uganda were of Indo-Pak origin, Britain could also have entered into some meaningful discussions with the countries of India and Pakistan in looking objectively at the whole issue of the national status of the Asians in Uganda. With some reasonable financial inducement several thousand Asians in Uganda would have chosen eventual permanent settlement in India and Pakistan and would have reverted to the nationalities of their countries of origin. India and Pakistan on their own would have certainly refused to accept any responsibility for the British Asians of Uganda. The Ugandan Asians themselves never talked on these lines because they felt greater security under the protective umbrella of Britain, and Britain for its part seemed determined to maintain its "greatness" by counting thousands of its erstwhile colonial subjects as British subjects, obstinately refusing to recognise political realities.

As the years passed the uncertainty hanging over the Asians caused their participation in the economic life of Uganda to become scratchy and hesitant. Their applications for Ugandan citizenship had become useless scraps of paper lying in the labyrinths of the Uganda Immigration Department. The political climate in the independent Uganda, particularly after the overthrow of the Kabaka in May 1966, became increasingly hostile towards the Asians. They were continually reminded by politicians from all parties and backgrounds that their days in Uganda were numbered. Milton Obote, in his various statements to the media and the public, made it abundantly clear to the British Asians that since legally they were Britain's responsibility they would have to go sooner or later, to make room for the Africans who were being promoted into various economic sectors of the country under several prominent government programmes. But he reassured those Asians who had legally become Uganda citizens that they would continue to enjoy equal rights with the indigenous Africans, and on no account would they ever be discriminated against because of the colour of their skin. However, he failed to give any ray of hope to the thousands of Asians whose citizenship applications had been frozen for years. It appeared that the passage of time and the adoption by Uganda of a new Constitution had rendered these applications void.

Meanwhile, to force out the British Asians and give effective form to the various government Africanisation programmes, Obote's government introduced legislation requiring all non-Ugandan citizens to apply for Work Permits, which were to be valid for periods of one to five years. Thousands of Asians who had given up all hope of acquiring Uganda citizenship applied for these work permits. Unfortunately, the processing of these applications progressed at a snail's pace, giving rise to further uncertainty in the minds of Asians. Applicants who were arbitrarily rejected were given three to six months to leave Uganda. The position of many Asian-owned business became so precarious that it was not uncommon to find many Asian family owned businesses part owned by members who held Uganda citizenship, part owned by members who held British nationality and were awaiting work permits, and part owned by members who had been given notice to leave the country. The whole Asian issue had been botched. Understandably, the Asians found it difficult to devote themselves wholeheartedly to their business activities. In this state they could not see much of a future for themselves and their families in Obote's independent Uganda.

In 1968 Britain introduced legislation imposing further restrictions on the entry of British Asians into Britain. Prior to this all British Passport holders whose passports described their national status as 'British subjects and citizens of United Kingdom and colonies' had the right of unhindered entry and residence in the United Kingdom just like any white British subjects born in Britain. Suddenly Asian holders of British passports, through no fault of their own, lost this right of free entry into Britain, despite their legal British nationality. Under a new quota system introduced in 1968 this new handicapped class of British nationals were required to apply for entry permits to enter Britain. These entry permits, or vouchers as they came to be called, were given out grudgingly by the British High Commission in Kampala, and the beleaguered British Asians were further humiliated by this 'special' treatment. The rush in applying for these entry vouchers built up steadily as the non-Ugandan citizen Asians lost their jobs and businesses under various government schemes, abruptly finding themselves without any sources of income. The rejection of work permit applications by the Ugandan administration increased the pressure on the British High Commission. Those Asians who were asked to leave Uganda were able to jump the lengthening queue for entry vouchers, and received preferential treatment in obtaining entry into Britain.

This then was the mess in which the Asians were in before Amin seized power. Consequently, they too heaved a great sigh of relief after the coup and joined the Africans in hailing Amin as the great hope of Uganda. Obote's regime had become alarmingly hostile to the presence of Asians in Uganda, and Uganda's news media had given prominent and supportive coverage to all such anti-Asian news. The Asians hoped that the change of regime would give them some respite from the unrelenting harassment they had been suffering, and would perhaps enable them to maintain their stay in Uganda. They also hoped that the new administration would be more pliant and understanding in resolving the long outstanding issue of Uganda citizenship for the Asians. So the Asians joined the black Ugandan civilians and Armed Forces in a massive demonstration of loyalty to Amin, and assured him in many ways of their fullest co-operation. These hopes of the Asians did not turn out to be entirely unfounded. Suddenly work permits started flowing out rapidly through the choked bureaucratic pipeline. The recipients of these work permits felt reassured, and soon there was talk of increased Asian investment in the economy of Uganda. But this new optimistic spirit was to suffer an early setback.

A few months after the military coup, when Amin had apparently consolidated his position in the country, he and his Ministers started making critical and often damaging statements against the Asian community, chiding them for not participating fully in the social and political life of the country, accusing them of various business malpractices like tax evasion, and condemning them for their resistance to integration with the black Africans - integration in the physical sense. The Asians were pilloried for apparently refusing to give their daughters in marriage to Africans. The mounting propaganda unleashed by the government against the Asians soon began to reach alarming proportions, but the beleaguered Asians, disadvantaged by deep and often irreconcilable divisions within their own community, seemed unable to check or alter in any manner the tide of events which threatened to engulf them.

Chapter Six

In October 1971 on President Amin's orders a census of the Asian community was held in which the Asians had to undergo a physical head count at various checking centres set up by the government throughout the country. In this unprecedented head count the Asians were required to give evidence of their nationalities by producing documents like passports, birth certificates and nationality certificates. This whole exercise, both in the manner it was ordered and in the manner it was conducted, was extremely humiliating for the Asian community who were being uniquely subjected to such ill treatment. After the count each Asian was issued with a green slip of paper as evidence of his or her as having been counted, and from then on was required to carry the green slip on their person at all times. The general belief at the time of the census was that Amin had ordered the exercise to obtain up to date figures of the Asian population in Uganda, with a breakdown of their nationalities. Very few people then imagined that behind this apparently innocuous exercise lay a sinister plan to transform the whole shape of the country.

The commotion of the Asian census had hardly died down when in December 1971 Amin announced the convening of a national Asian Conference. The District Commissioners of the various regions in the country were ordered to organise representative Asian delegations from their areas and send them to Kampala for the conference. No agenda for the conference was announced, but it was generally believed that President Amin would listen to the problems of the Asian community and enter into friendly and thorough discussions on matters relating to their general welfare in the country. The Asian delegations were hurriedly assembled, and the Conference was opened in an atmosphere of great pomp and ceremony by one of Amin's Ministers, Charles Oboth-Ofumbi, who was also to be the Chairman of the conference. After a brief address from the chair, the Asian delegations were invited to present their views.

Generally, and somewhat sycophantically (but forgivably in the circumstances), the Asian delegates lavished praise on Amin for his wise leadership and thanked him for convening the historic Asian Conference, the first of its kind in the history of Uganda.

They expressed the hope that the long outstanding issue of citizenship for the Asians would be resolved expeditiously, talked about their local regional problems and pledged their fullest co-operation to Amin's government in the cause of creating greater prosperity in Uganda. The Asians poured out their views with remarkable clarity and well reasoned arguments. The East African newspapers gave a detailed and generally unbiased coverage of the Asian views and the general consensus of opinion in Uganda was that the Asians had presented their case extremely well and with great clarity.

I was to lead the Asian delegation from my hometown of Masaka. Before the opening of the conference I had talks with leaders from the other areas. We agreed on a common strategy and I became their principal spokesman at the conference. In my address to the assembly I covered the main issues exercising the minds of the Asian community and impressed on the audience the strength of our case and the need for our total and continuing commitment to the well-being of the country. In keeping with the mood of the conference my speech was well received and our spirits remained high. We felt the time, effort and resources used in preparing and presenting the Asian case seemed well spent. We were in for a rude awakening.

Idi Amin made his appearance at the closing stages of the Conference. He came resplendent in his military uniform, accompanied by his cabinet Ministers and the top brass of the Armed Forces. The conference had been well represented by a cross section of national and international diplomats and dignitaries to this point, but for Amin's speech all the heads of Diplomatic Missions in Uganda, Judges of Uganda High Court, and leaders of all the religious denominations, journalists and other distinguished people from all walks of life were invited by the government to this session of the conference and, of course, duly attended.

Amin opened his address by unleashing a spectacularly scathing attack on the Asian community, accusing them of a host of malpractices. The Asians were stunned. Amin's diatribe completely ignored the views that had been presented by the Asian delegates, and the hopes that they had harboured for the amelioration of their lot in Uganda were shattered to pieces under the repeated blows of his accusations.

According to Amin, the Asians had systematically discriminated against African traders by refusing to lease suitable business premises to them in the urban areas, and where they had reluctantly leased business premises to Africans, these premises had been sub-standard and exorbitantly priced. This was why the African traders had not been able to successfully compete with the Asian traders and inevitably failed. Asian traders maintained two sets of books for evading income tax on a massive scale. The Asians were disloyal to Uganda, and were sabotaging Uganda's economy by smuggling huge sums of money out of Uganda. The accusations went on and on, but they were not just limited to the economic front. Amin bitterly complained that the Asians had never made any sincere efforts in bringing about a genuine physical integration with the black Africans of the country. Amin spent a great deal of time on this subject and challenged the Asian delegates to produce evidence showing the number of Asian girls who had married Africans. In some isolated cases where such inter-racial unions had taken place, he contended that the Asians had frowned upon them, and had often ostracised the poor Asian girls who had dared to enter into marriage with Africans. In a dramatic disclosure he read out a letter addressed to him personally from an Asian girl describing the agony and deprivations she had suffered at the hands of her parents, relatives and the whole Asian community merely because she had fallen in love with an African, and had secretly married him. (The original or a copy of this letter was never made available for further scrutiny or investigation.)

Amin's obsession with Asian girls was well known amongst the Asian community and it was believed that his rejection by an Asian girl to whom he had proposed marriage had inflamed his anti-Asian sentiments. (In the wake of these rumours it was seriously suggested in some Asian circles that efforts should be made to find a suitable and willing Asian bride for the President. Such a union it was thought would go a long way towards diffusing the explosive anti-Asian situation in Uganda. But the theory was never tested as no volunteer could be found.)

In his long address to the conference Amin did not give any hint of appreciation or gesture of kindness towards the Asians. No reference was made to the enormous contribution the Asians had made in building Uganda. It was as if the whole Asian community was being put on trial for crimes for which no advance notice had been given, and summarily convicted without being permitted to offer any defence. Only the sentence was awaited, and if the attitude of the President was anything to go by, the sentence was going to be punitive in the extreme.

The conference was closed with Amin's address. Afterwards the Asian delegates were invited to a State Reception at the President's Lodge in Kampala. Unexpectedly, some of the delegates were invited to express their views in an interview recorded for Uganda Television by Uganda's top TV personality, the highly respected James Bwogi. I and three or four other Asian leaders talked on behalf of the Asian community. It took a great deal of courage to openly refute some of Amin's more serious accusations against our community. Whilst disagreeing with Amin and neutralising his statements in a diplomatic and yet direct manner we also conveyed to the President our assurance that having recognised some of the shortcomings within our community we were prepared to work hard to resolve them until mutually satisfactory solutions were found. This recorded TV interview was to be shown on the same evening on Uganda Television. But it seems it was rightly calculated that the interview would have taken away some of the thunder of Amin's diatribe against the Asians so it was held back from broadcast for a few days. Instead, Amin's long-winded address to the conference was given repeated airings and by the time the interview was shown his hugely negative stereotypes were re-established in the minds of many black Ugandans.

Meanwhile, unbelievably foolishly, some Asians had laid on a most inappropriate entertainment for the President - an Indian dancing performance by a group of young and pretty Asian girls. The girls danced beautifully in front of the President and his Ministers to their obvious immediate delight, but the long-term consequences can only have been to further enrage Amin. To cap it all one Asian businessman took it upon himself to announce a gift of £6,000 to Uganda's Armed Forces - a huge sum in those days. The gesture took the Asian delegates by surprise and there were strong murmurs of disapproval to say the least. But once the announcement had been made no one dared express any opposition openly, and it was agreed that the money would be raised in the community to discharge the commitment (which proved to be no simple task.) Inwardly Amin must have sneered at such a gesture. Having accused the Asians of hiding hundreds of thousands, if not millions, was this crumb offered by the upstarts supposed to satisfy him? It would not be long now before he would take what he pleased.

It seemed that the whole affair had been an almost unmitigated disaster for the Asians and a near complete success for Amin. His plan to frighten, bully, humiliate and generally discredit the Asians was now well in motion. (When the time came these actions of Amin made the Asian expulsions all the more easy to enforce and palatable amongst black Africans.) The main purpose of the Asian Conference had been to test the unity and strength of the Asian community, and to totally discredit it in the eyes of the world by depicting Asians as the villains in Ugandan society. However, the outcome of the conference did not turn out to be entirely satisfactory from Amin's point of view. Whilst it was true that the Asians were initially reeling and humiliated under his virulent attack, they had got used to hearing most of these charges and had become almost immune to them. The African population too did not hear anything new in this regard. The coverage given to the earlier sessions of the conference by the East African newspapers and the sincere and spirited defence put up in the unexpected television interview also somewhat blunted the effect of Amin's accusations amongst the better educated Africans. Significantly, the President had learnt that the Asian community had a good measure of intellectual strength in defending itself effectively. Moreover, unity in the Asian community, which had always been almost non-existent and at best very fragile, had finally been made real and apparent. Amin was not happy with this outward demonstration of strength and purpose by the Asian community.

The President's mind was quick to grasp the fact that his plan faced a stumbling block. He had obviously underestimated the strength of the Asians. But this was not enough to deter him. On the contrary, he soon rearranged the situation to his advantage. In January 1972 he invited Asian leaders to a meeting at the State House in Entebbe, also attended by cabinet Ministers and senior army officers. I was present at this meeting and took a leading part in the discussions. Though we were not at this point in fear of our lives we were certainly anxious and did not know if Amin planned to continue the theme he had developed at the conference, but he surprised us again. The talks were conducted in a very friendly atmosphere. We touched on many issues and were able to thoroughly address the points raised by the President at the conference. We assured him of the loyalty of the Asian community to Uganda and our hopes of playing an integral role in further building its prosperity. We also acknowledged that some businesses indulged in malpractices and that we would do whatever we could to help in this regard. On the issue of physical integration we spoke of the need for patience and how the situation would evolve as the community felt greater safety and saw long-term prospects for themselves in the country. In particular, we told Amin that the community needed urgent reassurance of its place in the country if it was to settle again and provide of its potential. In return Amin assured us that as a result of this meeting he too now felt more comfortable with our community and felt that he now had a greater understanding of our hopes and dilemmas. He further assured us that in the future he would always be available to us and we would always be consulted on matters regarding the Asian community before he took any major decision, and to this end (we then believed) insisted we leave behind all our contact details.

The meeting ended on an apparently pleasant note and we were entertained to a lavish lunch. The champagne flowed freely and there was much laughter and joviality at the table. We felt relaxed and enjoyed ourselves. We had spent nearly five hours in the pleasant company of our now affable President and his apparatchiks. Indeed, we were honoured by the warmth of the reception accorded to us and initially felt very satisfied with the outcome of the frank and friendly discussion we had had with the President. After the meeting we felt elated at having made an important breakthrough in establishing a useful rapport with the President.

It is true that we were not absolutely sure of the underlying motives of the President, but deep down we were not so naive as to believe that we had succeeded in permanently transforming the situation in Uganda. As we debriefed in the Lake Victoria Hotel after the meeting we realised that despite Amin's friendliness and reassurances we had merely won a temporary reprieve for the our community. But we hoped that this easing of pressure would enable the Asians to organise themselves suitably for any eventuality. We were at least confident that an era of sordid anti-Asian propaganda was over and the community could look forward to a relatively peaceful period.

News of the meeting travelled fast in the Asian community and sighs of relief were heard all around us. But we had in fact played into Amin's hands. Our dilemma was that though we privately realised we were still living on borrowed time in Uganda, publicly we could make no such statements for fear of our safety. (Privately, I counselled countless individuals and families to wrap up their affairs, gather their loved ones and leave Uganda as quickly as possible. Many were able to peacefully continue their lives elsewhere as a result.)

Amin had realised that the developments at the Asian Conference had alerted the Asians to the perils of their stay in Uganda, and although they had been able to state their case fairly successfully, they could not have failed to come to the conclusion that their days in Uganda were numbered and that any attempt on their part to prolong their stay in Uganda would be detrimental to their interests. Based on this conclusion, the shrewd Asians were likely to further curtail their commercial and industrial activities in the country, and also accelerate the process of transferring the bulk of their assets out of Uganda by legal and illegal methods. Such a development would not only be a serious drain on Uganda's economy, but it would also leave behind very little of the Asians' assets for his Armed Forces and his supporters when they departed from the country. He had to reformulate his strategy so that he could hit the Asians when they were in a state of complete unpreparedness. The Asian Conference had put them on the alert, and the only way to distract the Asians and lull them into a false sense of security was to change his tactics immediately, but believably. This he managed skilfully by taking the Asian leaders into his confidence at the Entebbe meeting and then letting the country judge the success of the meeting by the changed attitude to the Asians. Some of his cabinet Ministers who had been known to habitually deride the Asians became quiet, and all anti-Asian propaganda ceased together with the harassment of Asians by the Armed Forces, Police and government officials. A period of calm seemed to have descended on the Asian community, and the period from January 1972 to July 1972 was one of the most peaceful times the Asians had known in the post-Kabaka era. Their confidence in Uganda became resurgent, and President Amin was praised and honoured by them once again.

While these events were unfolding Amin had been having some difficulty in persuading the British Government to expedite the release of the £10 million loan that he had negotiated with them. Amin wanted most of the loan released immediately in hard cash to enable him to strengthen and expand his Armed Forces, and also to inject some desperately needed cash into Uganda's ailing economy. The British government refused to comply with Amin's repeated requests, arguing that since the details of the loan agreed in principle had not been finalised, there was no question of any funds being released by Britain to meet Amin's immediate demands. Amin, who had repeatedly and publicly lavished praise on Britain for agreeing to aid Uganda with a £10 million loan, and who had taken personal pride in negotiating this huge loan from Britain, was infuriated by Britain's attitude. He privately threatened Britain with dire consequences if it remained recalcitrant. But the British government did not take Amin's threats seriously. They simply could not imagine that Amin, their protégée, was capable of harming Britain in any way.

But on 5th August 1972 Amin brought all his plans and threats together and hit at Britain's Achilles heel in

Uganda, the British Asians. In a well prepared statement he announced that he was launching an "economic war" in Uganda, aimed at transferring the control of Uganda's economy from the hands of the Asians into the hands of the black people of the country, and as a consequence of this all the British Asians would have to leave Uganda. He ordered the expulsion of all the British Asians within ninety days. He told the Asians that they would have to make their own arrangements to leave Uganda within the period of the ninety day ultimatum, and warned that those who did not do so would be forcibly removed from their homes and herded into special camps prepared for them by his government. This announcement hit the Asian community like a bombshell and put the whole community into a state of stupefaction. They could not believe their ears, and did not know what to do. The British High Commission in Kampala sought clarification from the government of Uganda on the precise implications of this totally unexpected policy announcement. In reply, Amin made it abundantly clear that the British Asians, and the other non-Ugandan citizen Asians would have to go in ninety days, and he was not prepared, under any circumstances, to make any concessions. However, those British Asians who were vital to Uganda's services like teaching, medicine and engineering were given the option to stay provided they successfully applied to the Ugandan immigration authorities to stay.

Britain's immediate reaction was that they would not be able to take into Britain all the British Asians affected by the expulsion order within the ninety day period, as their entry to Britain would continue to be strictly regulated by the quota system of entry vouchers under which only a limited number of Asians were allowed into Britain every year. The beleaguered Asians, stunned by the brutality of Amin's bolt from the blue, were now thrown into a state of panic by Britain's heartless reaction. In this dire situation, they could see not only the looming tragedy of loosing everything they had earned during a lifetime of hard work, but a terrifying threat to their lives and the honour of their women.

Men, women and children started forming long queues outside the British High Commission in Kampala desperately trying to obtain entry vouchers to their supposed homeland, Britain. The staff at the British High Commission proved quite inadequate in dealing with the avalanche of paperwork with which they were suddenly engulfed. The Asians slept overnight, often without food or shelter, outside the buildings of the British High Commission. Instead of showing any compassion towards these Asians who had become innocent victims of Amin's diabolical plot and Britain's folly, Britain behaved in an abominable and callous fashion towards its own citizens for no other reason than the colour of skin. (Imagine the reaction to such an order given against white British citizens.) There was not even a hint of assurance from the British government that the British Asians would be given some measure of protection in the event of any danger to their lives or that measures would be taken to ensure their entry into Britain by the deadline set by Amin. Instead there was a lot of talk of logistics. Britain wanted the world to believe that with the best of intentions and every effort, the British Asians of Uganda could not be flown out of Uganda by Amin's deadline.

A few days after his dramatic announcement ordering the expulsion of Asians, Amin invited the Asian leaders, the High Commissioners of Britain and India, and the Ambassador of Pakistan to his Command Post in Kololo, ostensibly to throw some further light on the economic war that he had launched. Members of the local and foreign press were also prominently present. He entertained all his guests to a lunch on the rooftop of his famous house, and talked amiably with everyone. Whilst the Asian leaders were understandably crestfallen, Amin revelled in the limelight of the publicity that his recent announcement on the fate of the British Asians had brought him. After the lunch he read a prepared statement on the Asian issue, and answered questions put to him by the journalists. The British High Commissioner Richard Slater also asked some questions, seeking clarification of some points in Amin's statement. Both the contents of the prepared statement and the answers to the various questions indicated that there was no change in Amin's policy. He stuck firmly to his avowed aim of freeing Uganda from the supposed bondage of Asian economic domination, and he reiterated his determination not to be swayed from the stand he had taken. The meeting served no useful purpose for the Asians. It simply exposed their pathetic helplessness. I was present at the lunch and was seated directly opposite Amin. I remember making some small talk with him and the others near me. I had been urged by some of my friends to raise some points with the President, but after listening to his prepared statement and the few answers he gave to the journalists and the British High Commissioner, I realised that Amin was not prepared to make any concessions and that it would be futile to ask him any questions. Besides, I did not wish to attract any special attention to myself.

After this fruitless meeting I quietly made my way home. I was deeply depressed by what I had seen and heard and knew then that that was the end for the Asians in Uganda. Like countless other thousands I had been caught unprepared. Just eight days previously I had told my wife that the time had come for us to wind up our affairs and decide on a new home somewhere in the world. But I had miscalculated and left it too late. Now I was in the desperate situation that I had been warning others against for months. My thoughts turned to what I was going to do get myself and my family safely out of the country.

Chapter Seven

A large section of the British news media went into a state of hysteria at the prospect of Britain having to accept these unwanted British citizens, who according to their various estimates numbered over 60,000 out of an estimated total Asian population of 80,000 in Uganda. They argued that it was inconceivable for a small country like Britain (population then around 55 million) to admit into the country such a large number of refugees in such a short space of time, and repeatedly warned about the adverse effect on race relations of such an influx into the country. This attitude of the British news media gave rise to genuine fear and panic in the hearts of many indigenous white British nationals, especially in areas like Birmingham, Bradford, Leicester and Southall which all already had large 'coloured' immigrant populations. In order to discourage the settlement of these expelled Asians in their city Leicester City Council took the unprecedented step of passing a resolution advising the refugees from Uganda not to come to their city for settlement. They claimed that their housing, education and social services had no capacity for accommodating any influx of refugees, and that they had more than their fair share of the burden of coloured immigrants. They told them through large advertisements inserted in a prominent Uganda newspaper to accept the advice of the Uganda Resettlement Board which had earlier publicised the difficulties of attempting to resettle in certain areas of Britain.

> 'The Labour-controlled Leicester City Council yesterday had a half-page advertisement in a Kampala daily newspaper, the UGANDA ARGUS, urging expelled Asians not to settle in Leicester. In large, black type, the advertisement read: "In the interest of yourself and those of your family you should accept the advice of the Uganda Resettlement Board and not to come to Leicester." ' - Leicester Mercury, 1972

Since the City Council was telling the Asian refugees not to come to their city, there was no question of any housing facilities being offered to them. Several local authorities in Britain did agree to allocate housing to the incoming Asian refugees, but the Leicester City Council officially decided against it. The anti-Asian tone of Leicester City Council was echoed by some other local authorities within the county. "Oadby has no room for any Ugandan Asian, declared Councillor J. B. S. Voss at last night's meeting of Oadby Urban Council Finance & General Purposes Committee" - Leicester Mercury, 1972. Even some of the leaders of the local Asian community in Leicester became pressured by the massive campaign against allowing the Ugandan Asians into Leicester, and talked about diverting these refugees to other cities! Such behaviour by a British local government authority was not only crass but also grossly inhumane, and ultimately and ironically futile. Rather than taking heed of Leicester City Council's adverts in the Ugandan press, many Ugandan Asians were informed of a destination where there was already a significant Asian community in Britain and made it their first choice for possible resettlement, accounting for the large Ugandan Asian community which now exists there.

It is hard to understand how in Leicester City a majority of its Councillors and Aldermen supported by a battery of so-called experts could not comprehend the fact, despite being reminded by some saner voices of reason and compassion within the Council, that the British Asians who had suddenly acquired the status of refugees, were not leaving Uganda of their own volition, but were being literally hounded out of the country with colossal losses. Never mind that the situation was largely precipitated by the British government's inability to find a negotiated solution to the crisis with Amin. Had Britain been less reluctant in parting with some cash in the form of an immediate loan or aid to Uganda and had they been able to understand Amin better, the Asian crisis could have been averted. Even after Amin's dramatic announcement ordering the expulsion of Asians, if the British government had reacted swiftly and positively the situation could have been contained, enabling Britain to arrive at a negotiated settlement for a phased and orderly evacuation of the British Asians over a reasonable period of time.

After its initial negative reaction Britain did make a half-hearted attempt to get some negotiations going by despatching Mr Geoffrey Rippon, the Chancellor of the Duchy of Lancaster, to see Amin. However, in President Amin's estimation Mr Rippon was not a Minister of sufficient stature, and therefore he was not prepared to enter into any meaningful dialogue with him. Even the British press wondered why Rippon was being sent out instead of Sir Alec Douglas Home, the Foreign Secretary. Shortly before Rippon took off for Entebbe on Saturday 12th August 1972 Amin informed the British government that he would be unable to see him before Tuesday 15th August. Despite this obvious rebuff, possibly caused by Amin wanting little more time to assess the British government's true intentions behind this move, Rippon arrived in Uganda as scheduled, but he did not manage to see Amin, and after a brief stay in Kampala during which he had discussions with some members of the Asian and white British communities he flew to Tanzania. Perhaps as a gesture of goodwill or perhaps out of curiosity to find out if Rippon had anything to offer, President Amin offered to see Rippon on his way back from Tanzania. The offer was promptly accepted, and Rippon broke his journey at Entebbe for a meeting with Amin. But the meeting produced no results and Amin remained firm in his determination to carry out his "economic war" against the Asians to its final conclusion. Britain's half-hearted efforts in seeking negotiations with Amin ended ignominiously. Britain's repeated protestations that they could not let in all the British Asians within the ninety days ultimatum had made no impression on Amin's resolve.

As hopes of any concessions from Amin petered out the British government seemed to become resigned to the fact that somehow all the Ugandan British Asians who had nowhere else to go would have to be allowed entry into Britain. Accordingly, the British High Commission in Kampala finally got geared up to tackling the mountain of paperwork that was involved in granting entry permits to the departing British Asians. But even at this stage the British High Commission failed to assure the Asians that the British government would evacuate them in time. The cloud of uncertainty, occasionally lifting to give terrible visions of tragedy, continued to hang over our heads. We lived in constant fear for our lives and shuddered to think what our fate would be if we did not get out of Uganda in time.

On the other hand the white British community in Uganda, some 3000 to 4000, were treated quite differently. When they expressed anxiety about their safety in Uganda because of the mounting anti-British sentiments in the country they were assured by the British High Commission that they had nothing to fear as the British government had made satisfactory contingency plans to deal with any situation which threatened their lives and property. They were further assured that in the event of any serious danger to their lives, they would be evacuated by helicopters from their places of residence, and that there was therefore no need for them to panic. All the white British nationals were advised to remain at their normal places of residence and continue normally with their daily work.

The white British nationals were small in numbers with little at stake, whereas the British Asians numbered thousands and had everything at stake. It was a sad commentary on Britain's attitude towards the British

Asians. In fact, it was a blatant act of discrimination, but there was nowhere and no-one to complain to about this obvious injustice. Most Asians were completely bewildered by the shock of the events and were in total disarray. Their main concern was to flee Uganda with their lives, and nothing else mattered. Such was the terror Amin had struck into their hearts, and such was their predicament with no country offering them any protection.

The British press had given a grossly exaggerated picture of the Asian numbers in Uganda. As the days passed and their figures were questioned, they had to revise these estimates downwards. From initial estimates of over 60,000, more reasonable figures of around 40,000 began to emerge. Of these some 15,000 were Ugandan citizens according to Amin's census figures. With the exception of a few hundred Indians and Pakistanis, the other 25,000 were all British subjects. In dealing with these not so alarming numbers under circumstances which called for speed and compassion, the British authorities insisted on putting the British Asians (who held full British Passports issued by the British High Commission in Kampala) through every bureaucratic harassment of applying and then waiting several anxious days for entry certificates. British Asians had to queue up for days outside the British High Commission buildings, quietly taking the sarcasm and insults coming from passing black Africans. The humane choice of dispensing altogether with the un-necessary permit applications and allowing free entry to all British Asians was barely given any consideration - apparently full British passports issued by legitimate British authorities were insufficient. At the very least, if for some strange reason it really was absolutely necessary that the British passports of the Ugandan British Asians had to be stamped with entry certificates, this should have been done at the point of entry in Britain. Then, instead of wasting precious time queuing outside the British High Commission for days on end to obtain these entry certificates, arrangements could have been made to organise business and private affairs and more could have been salvaged, and the browbeaten Asians could have been spared some measure of dignity. The unrestricted entry of British Asians from Uganda may well have let through the net a few doubtful cases but because of the very small numbers involved this would have been a small price to pay for the mental and material well-being of the new incoming British residents, oddly destined to be refugees in their own country.

A few days after his first expulsion order against non-Ugandan citizen Asians, Amin extended the expulsion order to cover all the Asians of Uganda, even those who were Ugandan citizens by birth or registration. This came as a rude shock to the thousands involved, mainly the followers of Aga Khan, the Ismailis.

The Ismailis are a sect of Shia Islam who believe the Aga Khan is a descendent of Prophet Muhammad in an unbroken line. They give him their full allegiance. Indeed their absolute faith in him in all spiritual and temporal matters can seem astonishing to the uninitiated. This phenomenal faith in the Aga Khan, also referred to as "Hazar Imam" (the present living spiritual head), has been largely responsible for the enviable advancement of the Ismaili community in many parts of the world. In the period of Uganda's struggle for independence the Aga

Khan had advised his followers to identify themselves fully with the indigenous people in all their aspirations by becoming their fellow citizens, and by working in close co-operation with them. As a consequence of this advice, which for the followers of the Aga Khan was a fiat, almost the whole Ismaili community had become Ugandan citizens. This directive of the Aga Khan proved to be very sound and materially profitable for the Ismailis. Whilst the non-Ugandan Asians lost more and more trading rights under government legislation passed by the oppressive Obote regime, the highly enterprising Ismailis increased their economic prosperity enormously by retaining their right to trade freely throughout the country. The Aga Khan also backed his advice with massive financial aid for his followers, facilitating their active participation in all spheres of the country, especially targeting education, health and industry. At one time, before Amin came to power, the Ismaili community had even made a cautious but ultimately unsuccessful effort to actively encourage inter-marriage between their girls and the Africans. Because of this positive approach the Ismailis as a community were considerably more successful than the other Asian groups in identifying themselves with the Africans, and the African politicians in turn liked the Ismaili approach. Their progressive attitude brought the Ismailis huge dividends in the economic field, and enhanced their image in the eyes of the general public. Amin's announcement of 5th August 1972 did not initially spell any great hardship for this well-entrenched community. On the contrary, many of them believed that the departure of the non-Ugandan Asians would give them more opportunities in business, and they eagerly looked forward to the departure of the British Asians. But their hopes were dashed.

When Amin saw that his expulsion order of 5th August did not provoke any serious economic or political retaliation against Uganda from any quarters he instigated the next phase of his plan and ordered the expulsion of all the Asians, irrespective of their nationality. This new order finally evoked some strong condemnation of Amin from many countries, including some African countries, notably Tanzania and Zambia. The Student Union of Makerere University protested loudly at this act of blatant discrimination against Asian Ugandan citizens. The previously emboldened Amin had not expected such a strong reaction, particularly amongst black Africans, and appeared somewhat disturbed by it. He was forced by some African states and sane African opinion to rethink his latest overtly discriminatory action. He had finally succeeded in embarrassing large sections of indigenous Africa, particularly the African states that complained and campaigned against the racial discrimination in South Africa and Rhodesia.

But apart from his desire to teach Britain an unforgettable lesson as punishment for its intransigence over the loan aid, Amin genuinely wanted to strike a lethal blow against the whole (in his eyes, upstart) Asian community. His ongoing criticisms of their activities and behaviour had made no provision for their national status. In his mind there was no distinction and he had no intention of allowing a few thousand Asians to remain behind in Uganda, merely because they had acquired pieces of paper describing them as Ugandan citizens. Nevertheless, he understood that the public announcement kicking out his own citizens was backfiring and that he had made an error of judgement. His response may have seemed a public retreat but was in fact no more than a practical and astute change of strategy. The Asian Uganda citizens were not going to be expelled, but in order to establish the legality of their Uganda citizenship they were to be subjected to a more stringent verification of their documents. Passports, Ugandan citizenship certificates, birth certificates and any other relevant documents would now have to be validated by the Ugandan immigration authorities. Under the new rules each individual was required to present himself or herself with the relevant documents at the appropriate government offices. This created a new mini panic amongst those holding Uganda citizenship. They rushed to have their documents validated. More queues of more Asians. Long lines formed outside the Uganda Immigration offices and the Registry of Births. The difference this time was the prominence of the Ugandan Armed Forces, who needed little encouragement to assault, abuse and generally insult the defenceless and cowering Asians.

The officers carrying out the verification of the documents were extremely heavy handed. In completely unprovoked frenzies of anger they tore up hundreds of passports belonging to the Asians, declaring that the documents were not valid and had been fraudulently obtained. Birth certificates legally issued in Uganda during the British rule were not validated for petty clerical lapses. Any imaginable excuse was used for non-validation and the newly dispossessed could only wring their hands in desperation and bewilderment. The debacle of the once powerful and proud Asian community progressed swiftly and satisfactorily for Amin. Vanquished and humiliated, they lay prostrate on the ground pleading for mercy from Amin. But Amin was determined to utterly crush them under his heel. To enjoy the spectacle of their humiliation and degradation he used to drive around Kampala in his open Jeep and watch the long queues of Asian men, women and children pleading with his petty officials for favours. The spectacle of Asian women and young girls being teased, taunted and molested by his African officers seemed to give him particular pleasure. Many Asians were willing to pay any price to prolong their stay in Uganda with a view to salvaging what they could in the aftermath of the crisis, but Amin's mind was made up and he was not going to bend an inch.[2*] The Asians were dispensable in his greater dream of transforming Uganda into a front ranking African country in which the black indigenous people were in control of their own economy. Still,

---

[2*] It must be said to the credit of the Ugandan African Christian and Muslim religious leaders that on hearing of Amin's expulsion order they had immediately sought an urgent meeting with the President to express their concerns. At this meeting, whilst expressing their full appreciation of Amin's policy of Africanising Uganda's economy, they expressed concern at the harshness of the expulsion order, especially with regard to the great suffering that would be inflicted on the Asians in complying with the ninety day ultimatum. In their naivety they pleaded with the President to give the Asians an extension of time to ensure their orderly and humane departure. But Amin angrily silenced them by telling them that his mind was made up on the issue, and he would allow nobody to stand in the way of the fullest implementation of his decision. The Christian and Muslim leaders were greatly dismayed by Amin's reaction and the summary dismissal of their proposal. They had tried to plead for some limited help for the Asian community but they had failed miserably. Because of their fear of the repercussions of Amin's wrath they could say or do no more. After this first and last futile attempt to alleviate the suffering of the Asian community, they retired quietly into the background, and could do nothing but pray for the unfortunate Asians.

despite all the obstacles, some 6000 Asians managed to obtain certification as bone fide Uganda citizens and won the right to remain in Uganda. The rest were in flight.

The exodus of the Asians swamped all the airline offices in Kampala. Immediately after Amin's expulsion order many Asians began to flee Uganda to anywhere they could go. Flights were fully booked for weeks ahead. Again the distraught Asians were caught in long queues outside the offices of airlines. To make matters worse the neighbouring countries of Kenya, Tanzania, Rwanda and Zaire had banned the entry of the fleeing Asians into their countries, and all their borders were closed to them. The only way out was Uganda's international airport at Entebbe. But buying travel tickets was not a simple matter of paying the fare. Before any tickets could be obtained authorization was required from the State Bank of Uganda. This involved the completion of several forms with complicated questions on wide ranging financial issues, proving all tax matters - personal and business - had been settled, and then queuing again for hours and hours outside the doors of several offices, one after the other before approval. The completion of this exercise also enabled the departing to claim their paltry foreign exchange allowances of £50 per adult, the maximum amount of money they were allowed to take out of Uganda. It took precious days to get over this hurdle: more amusement for Amin and his officials.

Kenya, Tanzania, Rwanda and Zaire showed little compassion towards those running from Uganda. They themselves were openly hostile to the Asian communities living in their own countries and therefore little could have been expected of them.

A small group of Asians had decided to board the train from Kampala to Mombassa in Kenya for an onward journey to India by boat. The train coaches carrying the Asians were placed under police guard during their journey through Kenya to ensure that none of them disembarked on the way. The Asians were not allowed to get down at any station on their journey through Kenya, even to greet their friends and relatives who had come to bid them farewell. On reaching Mombassa they were escorted under police guard to their ships for embarkation. Most of these Asians were British subjects who had decided to flee Uganda while Britain was dragging its feet over making a firm commitment to allow the entry of all British Asians by Amin's deadline. They thought that it would be prudent to find a temporary haven in India, but they were to suffer untold miseries and tribulations during their journey from Kampala to Mombassa. Near the Ugandan border with Kenya their train coaches were boarded by soldiers of the Uganda army, who raped some of the women and robbed all the passengers of their valuables at gunpoint. By comparison the Kenya police guard were better behaved, indulging in purely hostile rather than criminal behaviour. In any case, there was nothing left for them to rob. On hearing of these harrowing experiences all the other Asians planning a similar journey abandoned the idea.

The tension in Uganda continued to rise and it was feared that Amin's soldiers, who were becoming less orderly and more power drunk by the day, would go on a rampage of looting, raping, and killing the Asians. But Amin knew he had to prevent this. There was still the possibility of provoking active British and perhaps international intervention if events spiralled out of control. The British Government seemed to have put together a ramshackle contingency plan for dealing with such a situation, but they were still hugely reluctant to become militarily involved. Amin knew exactly what the stakes were and was determined not to allow any British intervention. He ensured that the intimidation and violence against the Asians were contained within 'acceptable' limits as far as the British government was concerned. With patience and a measure of restraint the rewards for him and his Armed Forces were going to be absolutely fabulous - the vast treasure of the Asian assets running into millions of pounds. Idi Amin was not going to allow anyone to jeopardise his plan for the acquisition of this wealth. So, though there was widespread intimidation and maltreatment of the Asians by Amin's soldiers, there were mercifully few cases of out and out murder or disappearance, and overall the excesses were not deemed of a sufficient magnitude to provoke an intervention from Britain. Britain's attitude was that only in the event of macabre scenes of an Asian bloodbath in Uganda would they seriously consider any form of action. Amin determined this would not happen.

Britain made no effort to help the Asians evacuate Uganda. The British government offered no financial assistance to their citizens in their greatest hour of need. The fleeing refugees had to find all the money for their air passages out of Uganda. The cost was around £130 per adult at that time. With an average of seven to nine members in each three-generation Asian family, the task of finding over £1000 in cash proved extremely difficult for many Asian families. It must be remembered that not all the Asians in Uganda were affluent, and many had their capital tied up in properties, business stocks and various trading activities and ventures. Many found it difficult to convert their assets into liquid cash because of the worsening situation in Uganda, and had to turn to the charity of wealthy Asians and community organisations to obtain their passages. A handful of affluent Asians gave freely of their money. Britain on the other hand, which had a moral and an arguably legal obligation to evacuate its own from the terror of a military dictator, remained supremely aloof from the vital subject of transport for the Asians.

Britain's loud protestations that on their own they could not carry the burden of the massive influx of Asian refugees into Britain, and their pleas of help, especially to the Commonwealth countries, brought offers of help from Canada, Australia, New Zealand, the USA and some other European countries. The Canadians offered to take some 6000 to 7000 immigrants and immediately set up an office in Kampala to interview the applicants. The Canadian officers were most courteous, and showed compassion and understanding of the problems facing the traumatised Asians. The Canadian officials processed their applications speedily and the Canadian government laid on special Air Canada flights to fly the successful applicants to Canada at no cost to the passengers. The Canadians acted truly in the finest traditions of their country showing a very positive and sensitive approach in the face of a humanitarian crisis, and giving practical demonstration to their sincerity.

Whilst some other nations welcomed the refugees, strong anti-immigrant sentiments continued to surface in Britain as a result of the exaggerated and melodramatic coverage given by the British news media. This created a very hostile and unpleasant atmosphere towards the 'coloured' immigrants coming to Britain, and the embattled and displaced British Asians who had 'succeeded' so far had no choice but to enter a hostile Britain to escape from the even more hostile Uganda of Amin.

The Red Cross, under the auspices of the United Nations Refugees Commission, accepted responsibility for the huge numbers of Asians who had been rendered stateless by Amin's Immigration officers. These utterly dispossessed Asians were taken under Red Cross protection and flown out to refugee centres set up for them in various European countries. The certified Asian Uganda citizens also quickly realised the gravity of their situation in Uganda. Sensing the danger to their lives, most fled along with the other Asians. By the end of 1972 Uganda's Asian population, which had numbered around 40,000 at the beginning of the year, was virtually non-existent. Their businesses, commercial holdings, buildings, factories, homes, cars and vast amounts of cash and jewellery fell like ripe plums into the hands of Amin and his soldiers.

The daring economic war Amin had embarked upon was fraught all along with danger to his regime, but it had succeeded completely and cost him nothing. At a stroke he had dispossessed the Asians of their great wealth, estimated then at over £200 million, and transferred it into the hands of his own people. The Ugandan Africans were absolutely delighted with Amin's victory and looked forward eagerly to sharing in the spoils of the highly successful economic war. Amin's personal popularity reached dizzy heights, and he was looked upon as a hero by millions of Africans across the continent. No black African leader had ever dared, let alone succeeded, in such a sensational operation.

One might ask why did the economically powerful Asian community of Uganda not act more decisively and effectively when faced with the threat that Amin's expulsion order posed to their lives and properties? Why did they not initiate direct talks with Amin to investigate avenues of compromise? Why did they fail to impress upon Britain the imperative need for it to enter into more determined and meaningful negotiations with Amin, addressing in particular the catalyst for the crisis – Britain's refusal to release at least part of the ten million pounds financial aid promised to Uganda? And, in the extreme, why did they not attempt to bring about Amin's downfall? The Asians had in their community the financial muscle, the intellectual ability and the necessary contacts to do all these things. Why not gamble their wealth while it still existed by acting decisively, albeit dangerously, rather than remaining impotent and helpless, thereby losing everything? What had floored and quashed the Asians?

Amin's success lay mainly in his use of the element of surprise (having once lulled the Asians into a false sense of security) and the speed with which he executed his decisions combined with the intimidation and terror unleashed by his soldiers. But to fully comprehend the dismal failure of the Asians it is necessary to factor in an understanding of the basic structure of the Asian community in Uganda and its inter-communal behaviour.

The community was never a single cohesive unit in any meaningful sense of the word. It was a loose collection of different religious and ethnic groups, often culturally incompatible but generally friendly towards each other. To outsiders they all looked alike and hence came to be classed as one community. But the cultural and religious divisions within the community were often deep and difficult to bridge. The Asians had always lacked a strong central leadership and apart from times of crisis it was not easy for them to act as a united community. Many attempts had been made by various Asian leaders at different times to forge a true unity, but unfortunately the Asians had tended to follow the advice of their sectarian leaders, which was not always conducive to their common political and economic good, and was in fact often highly detrimental to each other's interests. Beneath the genuinely sincere outward friendliness amongst individuals there was much suspicion and misunderstanding between the various groups.

In response to Amin's expulsion order the Asian leaders did get together and agree a policy to initiate direct negotiations with Amin, but they seemed to have very little confidence in themselves or their ability to achieve any success. Amin had driven a wedge between them by putting the Asians into different categories for the purpose of dealing with them under his expulsion order. Instead of realising the gravity of the situation and its full implications, the Asians went about concerning themselves with their individual cases and assessing the impact of Amin's order on their own sectarian groups. The President's move was a very clever one, and those Asians who were relatively untouched by the initial order of expulsion failed to engage in any useful way with those under threat. Some were even of the opinion that Amin himself was a very fine person and had no ill will towards the Asians, but was being maliciously misguided by some of his Ministers who were known to be strongly anti-Asian. But there was a consensus of opinion amongst the Asian leaders that an open and direct discussion with Amin could ease the suffering of the Asian community, and it was decided to address a letter to the President requesting an urgent meeting with him. I participated in a crisis meeting held in Kampala. We had long and hard discussions about the situation, and I warned this secret meeting of the perils facing our peoples and the need to open an immediate channel of contact with the President. I was asked to dictate a letter to the President requesting an urgent meeting. The letter would be delivered to the President in Entebbe the next morning.

There were also subtle undertones in the meeting that perhaps as a group we should arrange for an assassination. There was no question that the sums could be raised and that the contacts existed. But no-one dared speak directly for fear of being reported. None of us could be absolutely certain that another would not make such a claim at a later date if it suited his purposes, or if he was cornered into a situation where such information might be his last item of value. Also, we could not be certain of the consequences of such an action - whether it succeeded or failed. Either way it might lead to even more bloody consequences for our people. It might have only returned the equally ruthless Obote or taken the restraints off Amin's soldiers. We could not pursue this idea.

By chance, a prominent industrialist at our meeting, the well known and widely regarded millionaire and philanthropist Manubhai Madhvani, was due to attend a reception at the State House at Entebbe that very evening. Madhvani and his family had made an enormous contribution to the industrialization and general economic development of Uganda. We requested him to see if he could approach the President with a view to opening up a dialogue with him. We still had hope at that stage that we could buy a little more time from Amin and enable our stricken community to make an orderly exit from Uganda. But Madhvani was arrested the very next day on Amin's orders. His sudden and unexplained detention put fear into the hearts of the other attendees at that meeting and understandably our concern became more focused on our own individual safety. Amin had a highly efficient Secret Service. It is not unlikely that he was aware of our crisis meeting and had forestalled our tentative move. The letter was never sent.[3*]

Avenues of assistance that might have been opened up by international intervention never emerged. Britain made no move to set up any serious consultations with the Asians, and because of the total disarray in which they had fallen, the Asian leaders themselves could make no efforts to initiate any meaningful discussions with the British authorities. India and Pakistan also could have made a valuable contribution in opening direct negotiations with Amin, particularly as India's voice was highly respected in the Third World and Pakistan had very strong links with the Arab world whose friendship

---

[3*] Madhvani seemed destined to rot in the notorious Makindye prison indefinitely but was quite unexpectedly released a few days later. No doubt the resourcefulness of his family had come into play again.

was greatly valued by Amin. As the Asians of Uganda were mainly of Indo-Pak origin, the countries of India and Pakistan had at least the moral authority, if not obligation, to speak for them. However, they chose to let Britain bear the brunt of the burden, arguing that since these Asians were legally Britain's responsibility they could not interfere in the matter. (In their defence both India and Pakistan were plagued by crippling poverty and this may have been the key in deterring them from any direct involvement in the situation.)

Finally, when all else failed, one or two began to talk again of the physical elimination of Amin. There were many African politicians and several dissident army officers who would have been more than delighted to see the end of Amin's regime, and several of them saw themselves as future leaders of Uganda. But by now Amin's terror reigned supreme amongst the Asians and the prevailing paranoia and mutual mistrust made such a move unworkable. In any case the opportunity had probably passed, for by this time Amin's guard was well up, having openly accused the Asians, Britain and Israel of plotting his assassination.

> 'A statement from Uganda Security Council, which the President addressed this morning said, "The British government in collaboration with British Asians and Israelis and some other western countries are planning to assassinate General Amin before the ninety days deadline for the departing Asians. This in order to cause confusion in the country, and give them time to put in a leader who will be agreeable to Britain to

keep the Asians of British citizenship in Uganda." '
- The Times, 1972.

Amin had taken the necessary precautions.

Amin's triumph over the Asians was a phenomenon and he basked in the glory of his greatest achievement. His Armed Forces, members of his family and close associates shared with him the large booty left behind by the Asians. The magnitude of this loot was beyond the wildest dreams of the recipients, and for this sudden change in their fortunes these people were deeply grateful to 'Big Daddy'. They lavished praise on him, and lionised him wherever he went. Amin's stupendous success in driving out the thousands of Asians and effectively handling the crisis enhanced his personal reputation in the eyes of the whole of black Africa, and his name become one of the best known in the world. He had won on all fronts. Through his callous action he had gained an infamous notoriety in the western world and massive acclaim on the African continent. As he had warned, he had taught Britain an unforgettable lesson. In addition to putting it to the enormous expense of resettling unwanted and despised refugees, Amin had severely dented Britain's international image as a country of tolerance, justice and fair play. And above all he had demonstrated to his black African brothers all over the world that the once mighty Britain could be bullied and publicly humiliated with impunity. His boasts of immortalizing himself in the pages of world history no longer rang hollow. And he was far from finished with the history books.

Chapter Eight

The cost of resettling the displaced Asians from Uganda ran into millions of pounds. Even though in the end only about 24,000 Asians made their way to Britain, at the time the cost was estimated at over £7 million. Unquestionably, in the short term it would have been better financially for Britain to have given Amin a few million pounds in cash as aid or loan in order to buy extra time for the British Asians. If the British Asians had been given sufficient time they would have converted most of their assets into cash, and would have left Uganda peacefully, without putting Britain to the enormous expense of providing refugee camps and services. In these circumstances, the British economy would have benefited even more substantially than it eventually did as most of the Asian cash would have been invested in Britain.

But, paradoxically, even in the short term Britain derived several benefits from the Asian expulsion. Amin's expulsion of the Asians had been a blatant act of racist discrimination; black Ugandans had discriminated against Asians on the basis of colour. This action provided powerful ammunition for Britain, South Africa and Rhodesia to dampen the repeated attacks by African countries of racial discrimination by whites against the blacks in South Africa and Rhodesia. In terms of discrediting the black man and making the racial policies of South Africa and Rhodesia look like lesser evils, Amin had accomplished for them what they could have never done on their own at any cost or by any means. No one could have rendered greater service to South Africa and Rhodesia.

If the Asian assets had been taken over by the Uganda government through a negotiated settlement, the British government would have had to make suitable arrangements for guaranteeing satisfactory compensation of the Asian assets. After all, when Kenyan independence had been finalised the British government had made satisfactory contingency arrangements for compensation payments with the white settlers in Kenya in the event of government appropriation of assets, and the British Asians could have justly expected similar consideration. But their sudden expulsion negated the possibility of any such commitment. This principle of compensation remained long after the Asian expulsion. When Rhodesia became independent and changed its name to Zimbabwe, the British government agreed a land acquisition/compensation scheme with Robert Mugabe's government whereby Britain would provide money to Zimbabwe for the acquisition of land from white farmers at full market prices. In effect Britain was to provide compensation funds for the white farmers. That this arrangement has not worked out satisfactorily in the long-term is another matter. (In the early days of this agreement many Rhodesian white farmers did successfully sell their lands under this arrangement at the prevailing market prices.)

Britain gained immediately and hugely as the significant Asian role in the processing and sale of its principal exports, coffee, cotton and tea, was decimated. From the time of their expulsion this lucrative business fell completely into the hands of white Britons. London was the established principal market for Uganda's cash crops, and under Amin Uganda air freighted these commodities to Britain on special flights, which on their return were loaded with large quantities of British goods including significant shipments of whisky destined for Uganda's armed forces.

After the inevitable period of economic chaos following the expulsions, settled British businessmen were ideally placed to fill the vacuum left by the Asians in all areas of the economy. They reaped a rich economic harvest making huge profits in dealings with largely inexperienced and naive African businessmen. Previously, the presence of Asian traders had not been conducive to Britain's trade with Uganda, especially after Uganda's independence. Britain had steadily lost its competitive edge in prices to countries like Germany, Japan, China, India and Taiwan, and the Asian importers who possessed keen business acumen had no reason to buy the higher priced and less advanced British goods. The Asian traders also generally acted as agents for the various British firms of wholesalers and manufacturers, and this arrangement tended to whittle down the profits of the British firms because they had to give significant commissions to the Asian traders. The British firms would have preferred to deal directly with the African traders (at enormously inflated margins), but the Asian presence thwarted their efforts in this direction. The African businessmen were inexperienced and mostly lacking any basic sense of economics. They were too easily convinced by some of the so-called British experts (including the already mentioned bankrupt former pub-owner) that the secret to their success lay simply in the removal of the Asians who, supposedly, stopped the black Ugandan from developing in business. These British experts openly advocated the uprooting of the Asians as the recipe for enabling the Africans to become commercially adept. Having been easily convinced the black Ugandans were also, unfortunately, all too easily exploited by British firms. After the Asian exodus British firms traded in Uganda with ever increasing profitability, and Uganda's imports came largely from Britain, regardless of price or efficiency. The final irony in this regard is perhaps that the Crown Agents in London became the principal buyers of Uganda's requirements on the British market, and the Navy, Army and Air Forces Institutes (NAAFI, which is the HM Forces' official trading organisation) through its Kenya outlet ended up supplying the Uganda Armed Forces with most of their requirements.

The expulsion of the Asians changed permanently the course of Uganda's life. The reverberations are still felt now. It is an episode that the Africans of Uganda still speak of, sometimes with fond nostalgia for the friendly and peace-loving Asians and sometimes with sentiments of intense hatred for their alleged economic exploitation of their country. These sentiments of love and hate oscillate with the fluctuating political and economic fortunes of the country.

The expelled Asians for their part still carry many fond memories of their long association with one of the most beautiful countries and some of the nicest people in Africa. Many still long for their old homes and lives. The relationship between the Africans and the Asians had been symbiotic. Both relied on each other, and both derived tremendous benefits from the relationship. It was a pity that they were not allowed to continue co-existing. After the departure of the original Asian population Uganda recruited thousands of Libyans and Egyptians, and later, Pakistanis, Indians and Bangladeshis to man its various public services. But the indigenous Africans developed little respect for this new class of administrator who were less communicative than the departed Asians, and had much less understanding of the needs and aspirations of black Ugandans.

Amin's friendship with the enigmatic Libyan leader, Muhammar Gaddafi, continued to strengthen. The Libyan leader had assured Amin of his moral, financial and military support in the execution of his economic war against the Asians and he kept his promise. He provided huge sums of cash to bolster Uganda's tottering economy, and sent Arab doctors, engineers, and technicians to help run Uganda's various services which had started stuttering ominously with the sudden departure of the Asian personnel. He also sent Arab pilots and soldiers to strengthen Amin's armed forces and give him personal protection. The Libyan leader saw in Amin a powerful Muslim ally who would exercise continued control in Uganda, and thus keep Uganda firmly allied with the Arab countries in their struggle against Israel. Gaddafi also saw an opportunity of spreading Islam more vigorously in Uganda through Amin. After the expulsion of the Israelis,

Uganda's commitment to the Arab cause had become a significant feature of Uganda's foreign policy. In the Muslim Conference organised on Amin's orders in May 1972 in Kampala, Muslim religious leaders from various Arab countries were represented in great strength. These partisan religious leaders showered praise on President Idi Amin for his apparently enlightened Muslim leadership of Uganda. In their enthusiasm for promoting Islam and with Amin's encouragement they talked openly of converting the whole of Uganda to Islam. Amin's efforts to project himself as a strong and dedicated Muslim leader were very successful, and he saw for himself an important role in the Muslim world. The various Asian, African and Arab leaders present at the Conference were delighted with the warmth of Amin's hospitality, and were undoubtedly impressed with his dedication to the cause of Islam. The Christian religious leaders of Uganda on the other hand were obviously unhappy with the strong pro-Muslim propaganda. Uganda was after all a predominantly Christian country with Muslims forming less than twenty per cent of the total population of eleven million. However, they were unable to complain openly for fear of reprisals. They knew that Amin tolerated no criticism and dealt very severely with his critics. He ruled Uganda with a heavy hand and cared little for the opinion of the western world, and at this point he had not yet directly attacked Christians or Christianity in any way.

To say the least, the Arabs were impressed with Amin's flamboyant style. They were determined to aid this new and powerful ally. Arab money continued pouring into Uganda, and their numerical presence also continued to increase. Amin's crowning glory came when King Feisal of Saudi Arabia, the custodian of Islam's two holiest cities, Mecca and Medina, and the richest of Arab potentates, paid a state visit to Uganda. It was a personal triumph for Amin, and he entertained his honoured guest with all the extravagance at his disposal. Feisal was held in the highest esteem by the Muslim world and his official visit to Uganda was bound to enhance Amin's prestige in these spheres. Importantly for Amin, it also gave respectability to his regime and blunted some of the strong criticism directed towards him from western countries.

Amin's growing acceptance in some quarters obviously served to encourage him. In a totally unexpected (though hardly out of character) move in late December 1972, after the successful Asian expulsion, Amin gave Britain another slap in the face and issued a decree nationalising some white British tea plantations. The British government immediately protested against this arbitrary measure. The swift and strongly worded reaction to the take-over of white British interests was in marked contrast to its earlier attitude towards the Asians and their assets. THE TIMES of London reporting on the proceedings in the House of Commons stated:

> 'Seldom have MPs been as united as they are today in their condemnation of General Amin's latest decree nationalising British-owned companies in Uganda. Sir Alec Douglas Home, the Foreign and Commonwealth Secretary, usually the most moderately of worded Ministers said that General Amin's action was inhumane, deplorable, outrageous and insulting. In his address to the House he went on to say: "we are

already taking the necessary steps to protect the legal interests of our nationals both individuals and companies. We have already given very careful consideration to the legality of General Amin's decrees affecting the property of British Asians whom he expelled, and we have concluded that to the extent the expropriation of that property has already occurred it is contrary to international law because it is clearly discriminatory. We have just received the full text of General Amin's latest decree and we are studying it urgently. We shall be considering the legality of these measures also. In any event we shall call on him to provide prompt, adequate and effective compensation for all British interests affected. I have also instructed our representative in the United Nations to bring the matter to the notice of the General Assembly today." '

In order to justify itself and not appear obviously discriminatory by its condemnation of Amin's nationalisation of the white British interests and its demanding prompt and adequate compensation, the government was forced to make reference to the assets of the British Asians as well! THE TIMES of London in a leading article also talked of fair and prompt compensation. It said: "The businessmen have some safeguards. Under international law they have to be fairly, promptly and effectively compensated - and on a non-discriminatory basis. If this is not done - and the Sudan is the precedent - they will be able to prefer claims against the products, such as tea or cotton, of their seized properties on precedent set by certain oil companies. The British government, however, has the greatest responsibility. If it reveals any reluctance to insist on such compensation for its firms or nationals the impact on Africa at large will be very bad."

When the Asians entered Britain they made enquiries at the Foreign and Commonwealth Office to find out if it was possible for them to register claims for compensation for their lost assets. They were told that no administrative machinery existed for this purpose and, therefore, such claims could not be filed. But immediately upon the white British interests being taken over by the Uganda government the Foreign and Commonwealth Office in London produced forms for filing compensation claims. One can only assume the forms had been previously mislaid. In any case these forms would not yield one penny in compensation.

Amin found another opportunity to bully Britain and inflict almost unparalleled humiliation on her in dealing with the infamous case of Dennis Hills in July 1975. Britain was to be exposed and humiliated as never before.

Hills himself was a person of little significance. He was a British national who had lived in Uganda for several years and been unemployed since 1973 when his contract as a lecturer at Makerere University expired. In an unpublished manuscript titled "The White Pumpkin" he had written that President Amin was a "village tyrant" who had harmed his people and Africa. Somehow Amin's men got hold of the incriminating manuscript and Dennis Hills was arrested. By the standards of Amin's

Uganda the book was "subversive", and Hills was accused of having committed treason. He was arraigned before a specially set up military tribunal and tried, convicted and sentenced to death by a firing squad. The only person who could show clemency and grant Hills a reprieve was the President, but Amin had other ideas. In the Hills case Amin saw an excellent opportunity to humiliate and extract substantial concessions from Britain. He loved to be the focus of international attention, and this was yet another opportunity for him to play the big role on the world stage and enlarge his own international image. Poor Hills apologized to the President for his act of indiscretion and begged for forgiveness. But Amin's mind was not going to be content with a mere apology.

The British government made frantic appeals to Amin for mercy. Amin's response was to ask for Britain's compliance with a number of demands as his price for pardoning Hills. His main demands were: (i) the supply of spare parts by Britain for the many British-made weapons of Uganda's armed forces, a large part of which had been rendered useless because of Britain's embargo on such supplies to Uganda since 1973; (ii) an immediate halt to the smear campaign which Amin claimed was being waged against him by the British press; (iii) an end to Britain's campaign against economic aid to Uganda; (iv) a visit by the British Foreign Secretary James Callaghan or the Defence Secretary Roy Mason to Uganda to enter into discussions with Amin.

These were difficult demands for British government to comply with. The idea of sending James Callaghan or Roy Mason to Uganda was viewed with considerable trepidation as Amin's unpredictability made an assessment of his real intentions very difficult. Having to deal with the problem of one hostage in the clutches of Amin was proving hard enough, and the British government did not wish to land itself in a situation where one of its cabinet Ministers become a second and an even more prominent and embarrassing hostage. Prime Minister Harold Wilson's pleas of clemency for Hills produced no results. Amin continued to demand compliance with his conditions, laying great emphasis on the importance of James Callaghan or Roy Mason flying out to Uganda with a military delegation to enter into discussion with him. If this last and all-important condition were fulfilled he virtually guaranteed the release of Dennis Hills.

Meanwhile, another Briton, Stanley Smollen, who was a small-time businessman in Uganda, was arrested on charges of hoarding essential goods and was put on trial before a military tribunal facing the prospect of execution if convicted.

The Archbishop of Canterbury, Dr Coggan, sent a telegram to President Amin. The Primate's appeal read: "I write to appeal to you to show mercy and compassion, qualities which are reverenced alike by Muslims and Christians, towards Mr Hills and Mr Smollen." Several leaders of friendly African countries, including President Kenyatta of Kenya, and some Arab leaders interceded on Britain's behalf. Although in his various pronouncements Amin expressed great respect for these leaders, he refused to budge, and remained adamant in his demands. He continued to assure the British government that if James Callaghan were to make the trip to Uganda as demanded by him, it was possible for him to return to England with Dennis Hills. The British Prime Minister then took the unprecedented step of getting the Queen to address a plea of mercy to Amin. He despatched this personal communication from the Queen to Amin via two special British couriers, Lt General Sir Chandos Blair, the General Officer commanding Scotland and the former commander of General Amin's old regiment the 4th King's African Rifles, and Major Ian Grahame, who was General Amin's own company commander when the President served in the King's African rifles. The British government's decision to send these two former commanders of General Amin's old regiment with the Queen's message was considered to be a particularly good move as both these Britons were known to be held in high esteem by Amin. Ian Grahame was a personal friend and an admirer of Amin. Since the January 1971 coup which had brought Amin to power Major Grahame had visited him on several occasions. In 1972 he had described the General in an interview with the Sunday Times as an "outstanding leader" and a "tremendous chap to have around". Giving his impressions of General Amin from his earlier days when he was commander of Amin's old regiment he had said: "He was brave, showed initiative, was tremendously loyal, and a great athlete. He couldn't speak any English except to say 'Good Morning Sir', but it was obvious that he got promoted fairly rapidly, despite the fact that he was terribly handicapped by his obvious lack of education." Wilson and his government seemed quietly confident of the success of their mission.

Only hours before the departure of General Blair and Major Grahame from London, Stanley Smollen, who had pleaded not guilty before a Ugandan military tribunal on charges of hoarding essential goods, was acquitted by the tribunal. On being acquitted he was taken before Amin who told him he was free to stay in Uganda. Justice had been done and had seen to be done, he said, and Mr Smollen's acquittal would show the world that justice prevailed in Uganda without discrimination. Amin obviously felt that these well-publicised actions would give him an upper hand in the Hills case by depicting him as a fair and just man.

As the two British emissaries carrying the Queen's plea of clemency arrived in Uganda Amin began his fun and deliberately absented himself from Kampala. This was no mere spoiling move: Amin was again displaying his innate political instincts by asserting his authority over the emissaries. He flew by helicopter to Arua in the north of Uganda, ostensibly to take part in a ceremony marking Africa's Refugee Day. After cooling their heels in Kampala for more than 24 hours the two British emissaries were flown to the north to deliver the Queen's message to President Amin, who was holding court in a tribal hut. Amin was ensconced on a chief's chair in his tribal hut, and when the two Britons entered the hut they had to stoop down in order to pass through the low entrance and then sit on the ground with Amin towering over them in his huge chair. This gave rise to widespread rumours that the two Britons had gone down on their knees to deliver the Queen's message. The arrangement in the hut was such that this would have indeed appeared to be so.

It had been widely hoped that on receipt of the Queen's plea, personally delivered by the two special envoys, President Amin would release Dennis Hills. However, to the great consternation of the British cabinet Amin turned down the Queen's plea for mercy and reiterated his earlier demand for the all-important visit by James Callaghan to Uganda. But in deference to the Queen's plea he put off Hills' public execution by ten days. Amin expressed great respect for the Queen, but regretted that he could not accede to her request, particularly because of the irresponsible behaviour of her two emissaries! He accused General Blair of drunkenness, rudeness and a total lack of diplomacy in handling the matter. He further stated that the two British officers were regarded as spies by his Defence Council. Amin's strange and totally unexpected attack on the conduct of General Blair and his accusation that the two Britons were spies took everyone by surprise. Getting even with his former masters always gave Amin a singular pleasure. He never forgot the incidents of his past life and was always looking for opportunities to avenge himself against those who may have placed him in positions of indignity or servitude. His scathing attack on the behaviour and the character of the two British envoys may have been his way of getting even with these two Britons who had once commanded him. Because of the special character of their mission, General Blair and Major Grahame were unable to defend themselves publicly. However, in the British Parliament they were praised by James Callaghan for having conducted themselves skilfully and honourably in the delicate task that had been entrusted to them. Only the outspoken MP Enoch Powell dissented from the course of action the government had taken. He wanted to know how and why Mr Callaghan had dared court the humiliation which had been inflicted on the Crown by advising the Queen to write to President Amin. He was advised that the Queen had acted on the advice of the Prime Minister.

It is unlikely that Amin had ever intended executing Dennis Hills. He was merely playing a high stakes game of nerves with the British government and enjoying their continued international embarrassment. He was confident that if he played his cards well he would succeed in getting substantial concessions from them, so he continued to threaten Hill's execution. However, the British government for their part thought him capable of carrying out this threat, and when it become clear to the cabinet that nothing except a visit to Uganda by James Callaghan had any hope of securing Hill's freedom, they reluctantly began to contemplate it. Fortunately for the British Amin found a way to progress matters. Sensing that an impasse was being reached, he realised that the introduction of a third party in the negotiations was necessary to break the stalemate. He brought in President Mobutu of Zaire.

Amin flew to Kinshasa, the capital of Zaire, under the guise of holding discussions with President Mobutu on the forthcoming Organisation of African Unity conference that was to be held in Kampala. He made his surprise move from there and announced that on the strong persuasion of his friend Mobutu, whom he held in great esteem, he had agreed to reprieve Dennis Hills, and that he had appointed President Mobutu as the intermediary for all further discussions on the matter with the British government. President Mobutu was authorized by him to deal with the matter in whatever way he thought fit.

This new development was met with sighs of relief by the British government and without loosing any time James Callaghan flew to Kinshasa in an RAF plane to have discussions with President Mobutu. After being assured by President Mobutu of Amin's good intentions, Callaghan flew to Entebbe where he was accorded a warm reception by Uganda's Foreign Minister. His meeting with Amin was held in a very relaxed and friendly atmosphere. Amin turned on his full charm and it was hard to believe that any misunderstanding had ever existed between the two parties. Hills was brought in, and in the presence of James Callaghan he once again apologized to President Amin for his misconduct and begged to be forgiven. Callaghan no doubt expressed similar sentiments on Hill's behalf. Hills was given his freedom by Amin and handed over to Callaghan. The British Foreign Secretary had after all been forced to make an 8000 mile round trip to secure the release of Hills despite every attempt to avoid it.

Although Callaghan had made a statement to the effect that in securing Dennis Hill's release he had made no concessions, it was obvious that Britain had agreed to enter into meaningful discussions with Uganda for resolving all outstanding issues between the two countries and assist Uganda in various ways. Callaghan described Amin's action as "a gesture of magnanimity" and the British government was deeply grateful to Amin for his act of mercy.

Once again Amin had humiliated Britain and in the process gained the admiration of black Africans all over the continent. Even Britain's most prestigious newspaper, THE TIMES of London, wrote: "Step by step he seems to be trying to make the whole issue into one of black and white prestige, of independent Africa's right and dignity against the obsolete colonial pretences. In humbling Britain he will understandably strike a chord in some African minds."

The Hills affair was a particularly personal triumph for Amin. The British who had been denouncing him for unbridled cruelty and who had repeatedly called him a murderer had found it necessary to plead for his mercy. These pleas of mercy had come not only from the British press which had previously portrayed him as an arch villain and ruthless killer, but also from the British Prime Minister, the Archbishop of Canterbury, the European Parliament, the Secretary General of the United Nations and the Queen herself. The irony of a renowned 'merciless dictator' being suddenly asked to dispense mercy from all quarters was not lost on Amin. He had magnanimously spared the life of Dennis Hills after a friendly discussion with Callaghan, having first opened Callaghan's way by his own successful international diplomacy. In Amin's mind the whole process of freeing Hills demonstrated to the whole world his mercy and skill as a leader and robbed the British and western news media of their usual grounds for pillorying him.

Amin had also again exposed Britain's racial bias. Hills was one white Briton whose life was at stake because of his own actions. He should have known better than to describe Amin as a "village tyrant" in writing or even verbally in the hearing of any person. Uganda under Idi Amin was not a western style democracy that would allow such a criticism of its leader. It was no secret that Amin was not tolerant of any attacks or slurs on his own person or his regime. Anyone who had the audacity to do so should have expected the dire consequences that followed. Britain mobilized all its resources to save Hills' life. Commendable and humanitarian action, especially in the midst of Amin's games and bullying. But would Britain have mobilised a similar effort to saving the life of a non-white Briton? Tens of thousands thought not.

After the successful mission of James Callaghan, the Anglo-Ugandan political relations which had been frayed since 1973 began improving. The change in the relationship was marked by an increased diplomatic activity between the two countries. Britain took an early opportunity to reopen the issue of compensation for the British assets left behind by white and Asian Britons. Uganda initially responded positively by setting up the administrative machinery to deal with the matter. But, despite a promising start, the new era of co-operation would soon suffer a perhaps inevitable demise as Amin was, in truth, no way changed by the affair.

Although outwardly Amin praised Britain and the British way of life, inwardly he had a deep-seated contempt for everything British. Whenever it suited him, and whenever he had the opportunity, he used the British for achieving his objectives, but he never had any qualms about dumping and ridiculing them after their usefulness was spent. He revelled in putting British noses out of joint in ways that particularly poked fun at their institutions, social as well as political.

For instance, the well-manicured golf course in the town of Masaka had been held almost sacrosanct by the British during their rule. The golf course was on the way from the town centre to the hospital and African villages in the suburbs, and since there was no footpath by the adjoining road, pedestrians sometimes walked on the golf course to avoid traffic hazards on the road. But regardless of any such considerations, trespassing on the grounds of this golf course was considered unacceptable behaviour. The slightest misuse of these hallowed grounds brought swift disciplinary action from the British authorities. After the departure of the British the local Municipal Council gave serious consideration to a plan for converting the large open space of the golf course into a prime housing area, but because of opposition from the central planning authority (which continued to be dominated by British expatriate officers) and because of the lack of any serious demand for new housing land in the town the plan never came to fruition.

When Amin came into power he found in the golf course a perfect place both for landing his helicopter and addressing the crowds who would gather in their thousands to hear him. He frequently used it for this purpose to the consternation of the golf enthusiasts who would find their games cancelled without any notice. Whenever the golf course was used for this purpose it obviously suffered heavy damage. Large shelters supported by heavy wooden poles planted into the ground were erected to seat the Presidential entourage and other VIPs, and the ground was thoroughly trampled by the milling crowds of people who gathered to hear and cheer their liberator. By blatantly violating and desecrating another bastion of the old British colonial way of life Amin was cheerfully displaying his contempt for all to see.

The Africans of Uganda never really took to playing golf in any significant numbers, and for them golf remained associated with colonialism. During their rule the British never encouraged the Africans to play golf (using African boys as caddies only), and in the post-independence era when they made attempts to get Africans interested in the game (with the selfish motive of ensuring its survival for their own pleasure), the Africans took little interest in this relic of the colonial era. Today the Masaka golf course is no more. It is maintained by the local authority as an open space available to all.

Chapter Nine

On one rare occasion an individual British subject did slip through Amin's grasp, though not at no cost to himself, and obviously not without suffering the usual rites of humiliation.

> "A former RAF bomber named as one of 11 Britons who knelt before President Amin last month claimed yesterday that the incident was carefully stage managed as part of the Uganda leader's campaign to humiliate Britons." – Daily Telegraph

Wing Commander James Cobb, then 52, was a well respected test pilot of Air Force jets. He had been awarded the Air Force Cross for his work in this field after World War II. The Wing Commander said that the eleven Britons had been unwillingly sworn in as members of the Ugandan armed forces reserves as they were frightened about what would happen to them if they refused. Cobb said the ceremony was a "macabre farce". He had been "invited" to take out Ugandan citizenship by another former RAF pilot and close aide of President Amin because he had been training Ugandan women pilots. Apparently, "Amin was pleased with me and that he insisted I must become a Ugandan citizen. We could not refuse. We would have been in trouble. You simply just don't refuse to do what Amin says in Uganda these days." He was told that joining the reserves simply meant that he would be allowed to use the officers' mess and be allowed other privileges. "We were ordered to line up and kneel while trotting out a meaningless oath. Amin was nowhere near us, but it turned out that by trick photography it was made to look as though we were prostrated before him….We were tricked. We got caught up in a situation which we never intended. Had we refused we would have been expelled or imprisoned, or made to suffer some other public humiliation."

Cobb strongly denied a Uganda Radio report that he and the other Britons had pledged themselves to fight in the Uganda Army against South Africa. "But I do recall that Amin muttered something about how nice it would be if we went to war for him." Cobb said he decided to get out of Uganda quickly when it became clear that Amin wanted him to help fly the MiG 21 supersonic fighters delivered by Russia. He said, "I am proud to be British, and I was not prepared to take anymore of it. Amin will go to any lengths to humiliate and use anybody with a British Passport. I decided to take advantage of a national holiday when their guard was down and got out, leaving everything behind."

Generally though, like the biggest child in the playpen, Amin got used to getting what he wanted.

Inevitably, despite always backtracking if circumstances demanded, he started to push too far. Amin wanted the Chairmanship of the Organisation of African Unity (OAU) in 1975; he wanted the position and he wanted the international stage it would give him.

The annual OAU conference was scheduled to be held in Kampala in July 1975. It was the usual practice to elect the host head of state as Chairman, but it was by no means a formality and Amin was to face an organised campaign to deny him the Chairmanship.

Though this campaign was certainly encouraged by certain western powers, it was principally mounted by the OAU member countries Tanzania and Zambia. The Tanzanian leader, Julius Nyerere, had a twofold particular and personal intense hatred of Amin: Amin had overthrown his great friend and fellow comrade Milton Obote, and furthermore Amin the Muslim had seized the leadership of a predominantly Christian country and there was now talk of turning it into a Muslim State. The campaign against Amin was mounted by well-educated, influential and highly experienced politicians. Their initial tactic was to try and have the conference held elsewhere, expressing strong doubts about Kampala's suitability as the venue, citing safety concerns and the problems of Amin's repressive military regime. But Amin easily dispelled these misgivings, sparing no efforts to demonstrate that Kampala was a safe and stable city able to provide for all the needs of the summit. The conference went ahead as scheduled in Kampala, and his opponents on this issue were made to look foolish as most of the delegates had nothing but praise for the excellent arrangements.

During a meeting of the Foreign Ministers of the OAU countries, preceding the OAU Summit, Amin provided a very unusual piece of entertainment for his guests even by his own standards. He was brought to the party on a chair carried by four white men who were residents of Kampala. In his inimitable style he was illustrating the "white mans burden". These white men were people of significance, and in making them carry him in a chair on their shoulders Amin was having another swipe at the white man's pride, and was demonstrating the new depths to which the white people had sunk in receiving favours from their new black masters. The whole plan was an unmistakable affront to the white race, and he and his black guests made no effort to conceal their amusement. These attention grabbing antics, allied with much behind the scenes manoeuvring coming on top of the failure to have the venue moved, meant Amin's opponents could do little to stop him being elected Chairman of the Conference.

Amin could barely contain his eagerness. He had been determined to become Chairman of the OAU because by chairing this prestigious forum he felt that he could show the whole world that he was a leader of significance. As with so many of his actions, his motivation was to prove that he was truly a man of stature far removed from the buffoonish evil tyrant of popular depiction in the west. To everybody's amazement, and to the consternation of his avowed opponents, as the conference progressed this half-educated man, continually portrayed as a clown and a buffoon by the press, was able to brush off all opposition. The Conference was a resounding success for him and to crown it all he was elected Chairman of the OAU for the year 1975/76.

Unsurprisingly, Amin's tenure as Chairman of the OAU was not to be without its dramatic moments. He saw the Chairmanship as the ideal opportunity to further his self appointed mission to rid Africa of all forms of subjugation and imperialism from left and right.

During the Angolan crisis Amin played a decisive role in blocking OAU recognition of the communist Popular Movement for the Liberation of Angola (MPLA) regime in Angola. In the face of strong opposition from the National Union for the Total Independence of Angola (UNITA) and National Liberation Front of Angola (FNLA) factions, the MPLA, under the leadership of their pro-Soviet leader Dr Augustino Neto, had sought the OAU's official recognition of its regime at the OAU summit meeting in Addis Ababa. Amin's strategy of remaining neutral first and then joining the reconcialists divided the two OAU lobbies equally, thereby denying victory to the MPLA delegation, victory which had earlier been confidently predicted. Amin did all this in the face of a strong push from the Soviet Union to bring about official OAU recognition for the MPLA regime. The MPLA was heavily backed politically and militarily by the Russians and the Cubans, and it was widely thought at the time that Amin was being foolhardy in joining the reconcialists as he himself was heavily dependent on Russia for military aid. However, Amin was not so foolish as to fly in the face of reality, and later after the summit when he realised that the MPLA's momentum had become unstoppable, as militarily it had become stronger than both the UNITA and FNLA forces as well

IDI AMIN: LION OF AFRICA

as having succeeded in obtaining recognition from a majority of the OAU members, he simply changed his policy and announced recognition of the MPLA regime. But by now Amin had seriously annoyed his Russian friends with his former stand against the MPLA and his various statements on the Angolan issue. The Russians had become Uganda's principal suppliers of military hardware and maintained a significant contingent of military advisors in Uganda, training the Ugandans in the use of Soviet-supplied weaponry. Amin's handling of the Angolan crisis and his intimidatory remarks directed at the Russians had caused them great offence and they had packed their bags and left Uganda, withdrawing all military and diplomatic interests. Amin was left wondering at the severity of the Russian action. He had taken his stance on the MPLA merely to please his good friend President Mobutu of Zaire who had openly backed UNITA and FNLA. Amin had had no intention of driving out his Russian benefactors. Clearly, the Russians were more interested in Angola than in Uganda. The Russian action was a severe jolt for Amin and for a short time he was left badly exposed. But he was anxious to repair the damage. He may have been foolish in his initial position but he knew where his real interests lay and made a quick about turn. The Russians accepted and were pleased by Amin's change of heart and it was not long before they re-established cordial relations with Uganda.

Amin suffered a far more serious setback to his power and prestige in the aftermath of the Israeli attack on Entebbe in July 1976. The whole affair had the effect of depicting Amin as a principal culprit in the hijacking.

This was somewhat undeserved because at no time prior to the Israeli raid did Amin have any intention of killing or allowing the killing of any of the hostages. It should also be remembered that the hijackers landed at Entebbe only after they were refused permission to land in Algeria and Libya. Therefore, there could have been no collusion with Amin in the planning of the hijacking, and despite much conjecture based on Amin's general political and religious leanings no evidence has been produced to this effect. Nonetheless, once the plane was on Ugandan soil it became Uganda's responsibility.

Air France Flight 139 was hijacked on Sunday June 27th, 1976 shortly after leaving Athens en route to Tel Aviv. The hijackers were five Palestinians from the Popular Front for the Liberation of Palestine (PFLP) and two Germans with connections to the Baader-Meinhof terrorist group. Their demand was the release of 53 militants held mostly in Israel.

Amin was undoubtedly sympathetic with the Palestinian demands, and his support for the Palestinian cause was already well known. He had firmly aligned Uganda with the Arabs against the Israelis in support of the Palestinian struggle, and had repeatedly and unreservedly condemned all forms of Zionist activity against the Arabs. When he arrived at the airport he gave a speech in support of the PFLP and supplied the hijackers with extra troops and weapons. Given his avowed closeness to the aspirations of the Palestinian liberation movement and his open espousal of the Arab cause, these in themselves cannot be considered particularly sinister actions. He could hardly have been expected to behave differently.

Idi Amin was in his favourite position – centre stage - thrust into the role of mediator between Israel and the hijackers. His eagerness to play the part was motivated by his usual desire to boost his international image. Once again he grabbed at an opportunity to enhance his own stature internationally by playing a central role in the crisis. He spared no efforts in performing as the diplomat attempting to resolve the crisis, and he displayed great concern for the safety and general well-being of the passengers. It was after an appeal made by him to the hijackers that 47 women, children and infirm people were released on humanitarian grounds. A further 100 passengers were also released after the Israeli cabinet formally agreed to negotiate with the hijackers through Amin. By 1st July all the non-Israeli passengers had been released (with the exception of the crew who chose to remain). The remaining hostages were transferred to the Entebbe airport building and placed under the guard of both the hijackers and the Ugandan military.

Whilst continuing the public pretence of negotiating with the hijackers through Amin, Israel was secretly preparing its military assault. They had an immediate advantage in this task as the airport and all its buildings had been built by Israelis before their expulsion from Uganda, so the layout of the area was intimately known to them. Its execution was nevertheless breathtaking.

Operation 'Thunderbolt' began on the night of July the third. Three Hercules C-130 transport aircraft escorted by fighter planes were deployed to make the 2,500 mile trip to Uganda. One carried the Israeli commandos, their supplies and medical support; the second carried the Israeli Brigadier General Dan Shomron and a black

Mercedes resembling Idi Amin's limousine; the third a demolition team whose task was the immobilization of Uganda's MiG fighters.

The Ugandan soldiers and the hijackers were completely taken by surprise when the three Hercules transport planes landed at about 1.00am local time. Around 200 elite troops ran out and stormed the airport building. In a tense 35-minute battle twenty Ugandan soldiers and all seven hijackers were killed along with three hostages and the Israeli officer who had led the assault, Jonathan Netanyahu. (Netanyahu's brother, Benjamin, would go on to become Prime Minister of Israel.) The Israelis also destroyed eleven Russian-built MiG fighters, a quarter of Uganda's air force. The surviving hostages were flown to Israel after a stopover in Nairobi, Kenya, where the injured were treated by Israeli doctors. The only hostage unaccounted for was Mrs Dora Bloch.

Mrs Bloch's disappearance was to prompt the breaking of diplomatic relations with Britain as well as the re-imprinting on the international conscious of Amin as a monster.

Dora Bloch was over seventy years old, Jewish and with dual Israeli and British nationality. Before the Israeli raid on Entebbe she had been taken to the Mulago Hospital in Kampala on the President's personal orders, in his official car, for treatment for breathing problems she had developed after partially choking on a piece of meat. Amin's gesture of kindness was no doubt partly motivated by his desire to portray a good public image. It backfired massively and tragically for Mrs. Bloch. After the raid when the Israelis failed to get any information on her whereabouts they accused Amin of having murdered her in a vile act of revenge. There were reports that Amin had directed his officers to get her out of the hospital and take her to an unknown destination where she had been murdered. Amin steadfastly denied any knowledge of her whereabouts and stated that since the Israelis had taken over the responsibility for the hijacked passengers he could not be held responsible for Mrs Bloch's fate. In reply to all the enquiries raised by Britain he told them that they should contact Israel. Britain and Israel tried through all their sources to unravel the mystery of the disappearance of Mrs Bloch, but their enquiries led nowhere. After their unsuccessful efforts they came to the sad conclusion that she had been killed, and that her body had probably been secretly disposed off.

In the aftermath of the Entebbe raid, Uganda's relations with Kenya became very bitter. Because the Israelis had used the Nairobi airport for refuelling their aircraft on their return from Uganda and had also had full use of Kenya's medical services to treat their wounded, Amin accused Kenya of collusion with the Israelis in their attack on Entebbe. Amin alleged that Kenya had full advance knowledge of the Israeli attack on Entebbe. He further alleged that it had also actively assisted the Israelis in the execution of their plan. Kenya denied all the charges, stating that permission to land at Nairobi had been given only after the raid.

In the mounting tension between the two countries Amin threatened to invade Kenya. This was greatly out of pattern to the former relationship between the two countries. The President of Kenya, Jomo Kenyatta, had always adopted an almost fatherly attitude towards Amin and had helped him on several occasions. In fact, Amin had leaned on him many times for advice and assistance and Kenyatta had always obliged by coming to his aid. But Amin's new belligerent attitude towards Kenya proved too much for the angered Kenyatta and he came to the conclusion that the time had come to force Amin out of power.

Uganda is a land locked country and it depended on the Kenyan port of Mombassa to facilitate all its imports and exports by sea. Uganda's oil and petrol supplies came from the oil refinery in Kenya. Uganda was also heavily in debt to Kenya. Kenyatta decided to demand prompt cash payment in foreign exchange for all transport costs of petrol and other transit charges. But Uganda was desperately short of cash and therefore unable to comply. These measures by the Kenyan authorities were tantamount to an economic blockade, and the Ugandan economy was brought to almost a complete standstill. Petrol supplies in Uganda ran out, and the whole transport network, so vital to Uganda's economy, came to a grinding halt.

The Entebbe crises and all its consequences had been a series of devastating blows for Amin. The effects of the economic blockade were so disastrous for Uganda's economy that Amin might easily have been toppled from power. There was strong speculation that his downfall was imminent. For once he had been so roundly cornered that the only way out for him seemed his immediate exit from power. Senior army officers were so alarmed by the deteriorating economic situation that they plucked up the courage to broach the idea with Amin that he might step down in favour of a new military leader or a military junta that could immediately proceed to enter into negotiations with Kenya to break the economic blockade and repair Uganda's damaged political image. Amin listened to them and invited them to a meeting for further discussions. Suddenly and without explanation, there was no more talk of regime change after this meeting. Somehow Amin had once again surprised those who underestimated him. Probably by promising to deliver repaired relations with Kenya, he survived and turned the situation.

Immediately and quite unexpectedly he embarked on a new initiative to resolve his differences with Kenya. Despite all his bravado and muscle flexing he knew that without the vital supplies of petrol his military was rendered useless and he could never invade Kenya successfully. He put his simple new plan into action. All anti-Kenya propaganda was halted and in a complete about turn he praised Jomo Kenyatta for his wise leadership and statesmanship and offered to open negotiations with the Kenyan authorities for normalising relations between the two countries. At first Kenya paid no heed to Amin's overtures, but in a matter of days a Ugandan delegation was in Kenya talking to Kenyan Ministers. As a result of the meeting relations between the two countries were restored and the vital petrol supplies and other goods started flowing into Uganda. With his position threatened Amin had done whatever he had to, defied all expectations and survived the attempts to force him out.

Chapter Ten

Domestically, Amin's abuses and terror continued. In 1977 one particular series of incidents brought him back into sharp and harsh international focus.

In January 1977 seven men were killed as Amin's forces put down a small army rebellion. But this was not sufficient for Amin. As usual his methods were ruthless and swift. Determined to stamp out all traces of opposition, thousands were killed under his orders within days and the population of Milton Obote's home village was decimated. A prominent church leader unable to hold back preached on the sanctity and preciousness of human life to an audience that included prominent government officials. He accused the regime of arbitrary bloodletting and abusing the position in which God had placed it. Amin's response was a raid on the home of Archbishop Janani Luwum, Archbishop of the Metropolitan Province of Uganda, Rwanda, Burundi and Boga-Zaire, on the pretext of searching for illegally held arms. The Archbishop in turn sent an open letter to the President signed by seventeen other Anglican bishops in Uganda protesting at the arbitrary killings and disappearances. Then on February the fourteenth, Amin produced a document apparently written by

Milton Obote that implicated Luwum in a treasonous conspiracy. Luwum and his wife were interviewed by Amin in the Presidential Palace near Lake Victoria. They both strongly denied the allegations against them and were advised by the President to restrict their activities strictly to religious matters. On February the sixteenth the Archbishop and two Cabinet members (Charles Oboth-Ofumbi and Erianayo Oryema, committed Christians and the last survivors of Amin's original cabinet) were arrested. They died the same day. The authorities claimed that they had died as a result of a car crash on their way to interrogation caused by a failed attempt to overpower the driver. Other sources spoke of more horrific endings. Luwum's wife and five children fled the country.

The killings sent shock waves throughout the Christian world. As a result of this brutality Idi Amin's regime came to be hated and opposed as never before. The Christian churches in Uganda were terrorised into silence but Christian churches outside Uganda took up the case with all their force. Even though less than 20 per cent of the population of eleven million were Muslims, the churches feared that it was only a matter of time before Amin declared Uganda a Muslim state and that the murders of Luwum and the two ministers were part of a plan to strike at the heart of Christianity in Uganda. They mounted a vigorous campaign against Amin specifically calculated to bring about his downfall. For the Christian churches the killing of Archbishop Luwum was the last straw and they openly urged the Western world to ostracise Idi Amin and bring him down. They threw all caution to the winds calling for regime change and even assassination.

1977 was also the year of the Queen's Silver Jubilee celebrations and that year's Commonwealth Conference was scheduled to be held in June in London. There had already been many calls for Amin's exclusion. This opposition to his attendance gathered real momentum after the deaths of Luwum and the two cabinet Ministers. By this time the British too could take little more from Amin. They had quietly backed him from the time of his coup for their economic and political gain, but they could stand by his excesses and unpredictability no more. In the mounting pressure to exclude Amin from the conference the British government switched to the moral high ground and embarked upon an intense campaign of diplomatic activity to convince Commonwealth leaders of the desirability of keeping Amin away. However, try as they might, the British could not convince most of the Commonwealth countries to denounce Amin. (Uganda was after all not the only Commonwealth country with blood on its hands and on top of economic and social considerations there was still a sense of solidarity amongst some African nations.) Still, when all was said and done Britain had the right to refuse entry to any non-British national and means were found to exclude Amin.

Obviously there were many reasons for cited for Amin's exclusion, such as his domestic repression and appalling human rights record, his public denouncements of other nations and his (somewhat successful) attempts to arrange an African boycott of Israel. One of the principal reasons given for debarring him was that his presence at the conference would divert attention from the important issues of the conference as he would inevitably become the focus of attention. But ironically, despite his absence the British news media devoted a considerable amount of time and space to Amin, and his name and image haunted the conference throughout its duration.

Although the Commonwealth leaders in their final communiqué condemned the "systematic disregard of the sanctity of life and massive violation of basic human rights in Uganda", they were unable to attack President Amin personally because too many delegates either voted against or abstained from naming him. It was rather a futile gesture and if anything counterproductive. Amin never forgot or forgave a slight of any nature. It would have been far better to ignore him completely. By excluding Amin from the conference Britain inflicted unnecessary hardship on its own nationals in Uganda, and also added to the suffering of the Ugandans who in some measure had to bear the wrath of their President. By isolating him and by condemning his regime nothing was accomplished.

Regardless of communiqués or other peoples' opinions, Amin continued to rule Uganda the way he had always ruled Uganda - through the gun. In the language of guns he was articulate. Guns had brought him into power and they sustained him, just as they had come to sustain Milton Obote.

Obote's years of government after May 1966 had seen the emergence of the armed forces as significant players in ruling Uganda. Under Amin they became the only force that ruled the country and whatever remnants of democracy that were left when he came to power quickly evaporated.

The fact that Obote's government lost its civilian power base, and came to rely increasingly on the armed forces to keep him in power, was not due to any conspiracy or plot by Amin. Uganda was another instance where interference by a western colonial power in the internal affairs and development of a country was to prove counterproductive and harmful to the long-term interests of its indigenous people. As was always the case, the colonial rule in Uganda had been motivated in the first instance by the selfish desire of the rulers to exploit the resources of a colonised country. In the beginning the exploitation was carried out blatantly, but later it was done under the guise of imparting civilisation to the so-called backward colonial subjects. Uganda like many others had had a long colonial tutelage but very little good came of it. The failure lay not in the incompetence or ineptness of the Africans but in the fact that the colonial power had paid more attention to teaching the Africans the framework and structure of their institutions rather than the spirit and philosophy behind them. Without this understanding they could never really relate to these institutions and acquire ownership of them in any meaningful sense. Without this understanding there was little hope but that there would be a reversion to absolute tribal models of rule, albeit manifested benignly or ruthlessly, and that authority would be maintained through force. To this day the armed forces continue to play a significant role in the political life of the Uganda. Mercifully though under President Yoweri Kaguta Museveni, who seized power in 1986 with his National Resistance Army and still rules today, the absolute model of power has been manifested largely in its benign form and has in fact served Uganda well.

With the armed forces behind him Amin maintained an iron grip on Uganda, indulging in countless acts of murder, terror and repression, crushing even any hint of opposition. Attempts were made on his life but each time he came through untouched. The 'buffoon' continually outwitted and confounded his enemies, any of whom would be lucky to survive their misdemeanours with their lives.

When Amin seized power most political pundits did not think that his regime would survive for more than a few months, but he remained in complete control of Uganda for nearly nine years. All the external attempts to force him out of power failed. By 1978 nearly every nation in the world had cut diplomatic ties with Uganda.

Still the hope prevailed that somehow he would be brought down. Because of the brutal nature of his regime and because he had ruled Uganda ruthlessly by the power of the gun it was often said (and hoped by those who had suffered at his hands) that eventually he himself would be brought down by a gun, dying a brutal and ignominious death. In the end though it was his own folly that brought him down.

Chapter Eleven

Idi Amin's downfall came in 1979 when he was driven out of power by the combined forces of the Tanzanian army and Milton Obote's guerrilla force that invaded Uganda from across its southern border in response to Amin's invasion of Tanzania.

Obote had sought refuge with his friend and ideological comrade President Julius Nyerere in Tanzania. From there he had for some time been building up a militia force with the intention of recapturing power. Amin was well aware of this and repeatedly threatened to invade Tanzania and teach Julius Nyerere a lesson. At the same time he called him a coward and challenged him using particularly insulting language. He publicly said Nyerere behaved like a woman and that if he had in fact been a woman he would have asked him to marry him! Also Amin had not forgotten how Kenya had strangled his expansionist ambitions simply by denying him access to a seaport, and he now seemed to be entertaining visions of acquiring a seaport through Tanzania by capturing Dar-Es-Salam, the capital and seaport of Tanzania.

In late 1978 with the Ugandan economy spiralling out of control and in the grip of rampant inflation Amin attempted to annex the northern Tanzanian province of Kagera with the assistance of Libyan troops. He succeeded in temporarily seizing a strip of territory north of the Kagera River. Nyerere swiftly mobilized his army and forced out Amin's soldiers. Amin had made repeated incursions into Tanzania previously but by now President Nyerere had been provoked beyond the point of return. He came to the conclusion, like others before him, that enough was enough and that it was time to put a stop to Amin once and for all. Nyerere would not be satisfied with merely repulsing Amin's forces as he had done in the past. He chose to combine his forces with Obote's militia and launch a full-scale invasion of Uganda. The invading force called itself the Liberation Army. It was large and well-armed.

By this time, those Amin could be certain of their loyalty comprised only 25 per cent of his army, who were Ugandans. The rest had been imported from Sudan and Zaire and also, of course, Libya. They fled in terror. Rumours that the invading forces had a voodoo induced invincibility had spread through the already non-cohesive forces and they were in no mood to test the point. The invading army continued its march to Kampala without encountering any significant resistance. (To demonstrate its strength bombs were lobbed at many buildings quite indiscriminately and quite unnecessarily. My old town of Masaka suffered perhaps the heaviest damage and destruction, being the main town on the path of the invading force on its way to Kampala.) The small force of Libyan soldiers sent by President Gaddafi proved to be quite inept and quickly surrendered to the advancing forces of the Tanzanian army and Obote's militia.

The reports were that Amin had been desperate to put up a fight and was reduced to tears when his panic stricken troops surrendered and scattered. When he realised that the game was up he fled from Uganda with members of his family and close associates to Libya where his friend President Gaddafi gave him refuge.

Amin's regime had been brought down by the gun, but he himself had escaped unharmed and avoided the bloody death many had predicted and hoped for him. He stayed in Libya until 1981 when he was given refuge in Saudi Arabia as a guest of the Saudi royal family, and he was provided with a comfortable lifestyle for the rest of his days. He lived a pleasant and relatively free life in the city of Jeddah in Saudi Arabia until he passed away peacefully in hospital on 16th August 2003 at the ripe old age of 80.

Amin made an indelible mark on the history of the world. He successfully translated nearly all of his boasts into reality. He even succeeded in emulating his hero Adolf Hitler by acquiring international notoriety through the expulsion of the Israelis and Asians. Like Hitler, who had made Jews the scapegoats for all the ills of Germany and exterminated them in the most brutal fashion, Amin found his scapegoat in the Asian community and got rid of them, having threatened to put them in barbed wire fenced camps if they did not leave Uganda within their ninety days period. Hitler is an enduringly and perversely fascinating character and Amin is also perhaps cast in the same mould. He will be remembered long after his death. His name had already entered dictionaries around the world prior to his death and his face is an iconic image familiar to millions across the globe.

He will not be remembered kindly. Estimates of the numbers killed under his regime vary between 100,000 and 500,000. The damage he did to Uganda and her neighbours is barely quantifiable. But by his actions he immortalised himself: he will not be forgotten.

His name and everything about him will continue to fascinate many people in the world. This poorly educated man became Uganda's President. Denied a formal education and twice denied promotion for failing military exams, by the time of his overthrow he was formally known as "His Excellency President for Life Field Marshal Al Hadj Doctor Idi Amin Dada, VC, DSO, MC, Lord of All the Beasts of the Earth and Fishes of the Sea and Conqueror of the British Empire in Africa in General and Uganda in Particular", not to mention that he was also Chancellor of the only university in Uganda. What he did not do, but I am sure intended to if he had more time, was to emulate his close friend Jean Badel Bokasa of the Central African Republic, whom he had described as 'one of the greatest leaders of Africa', and crown himself as Emperor of Uganda and adopt the title "His Imperial Majesty." Had he done so he would have certainly brought more ridicule upon himself from the western world. But in the African world he was and remains for many a popular hero because uniquely, and for a time successfully, he stood up to the white man. When he announced at the OAU conference held in Libreville, Gabon in July 1977 (the month after he had been excluded from the Commonwealth Conference in London) that the ruling Defence Council of Uganda had awarded him the title of CBE, 'Conqueror of the British Empire', he was met with thunderous applause from both the public and OAU delegates.

> 'President Amin of Uganda took the Organisation of African Unity's summit by storm last night, winning rounds of applause from his fellow African leaders as he publicly admitted for the first time that he survived an attempt on his life last month. There was no hint of opprobrium or censure of his regime and there was cheering and applause when he informed the Conference that his ruling Defence Council had awarded him CBE: "The Conqueror of the British Empire". There was renewed applause as he left the rostrum and marched back to his place around the vast horseshoe-shaped table.
>
> Amin, clearly the darling of the conference, was the last speaker, immediately after President Kaunda, who has a record of opposition to him. Amin's undeniable popularity among both delegates and onlookers in Libreville has caused some surprise among observers. Outside the auditorium that night, a young Gabonese student who was applauding Amin as the Uganda leader stepped from the car said: "I like Amin because he knows how to say 'no' to the white man". Another Gabonese said: "If there was an election for a king of Africa, Idi would be it." Asked about Amin's record on human rights another Gabonese

replied: "Look, let's be frank and admit that in every country everywhere there are leaders who have to take measures to save themselves. There is no particular point in singling out Amin." '

THE DAILY TELEGRAPH, 1977

What THE TIMES of London said of Amin in a leading article as far back as 1972 remains true for many Africans even today:

> 'General Amin's treatment of the Asians, the British, even the Israelis, it must be faced has won more respect than a censure in Africa.'

For many Africans, even today, Idi Amin was and is the Lion of Africa.

Epilogue

Whilst on a pilgrimage to Mecca in 1986 I had the opportunity to meet with Idi Amin again. The meeting was arranged by a close friend of mine, Dr Abdul Majid Qureshi, a fellow Ugandan Asian then a Consultant in a hospital in Jeddah, the city where Amin had taken up residence.

When the time came we were informed that we should travel to his villa. With warnings from our wives not to eat anything that Amin did not also eat himself and to generally be alert of any danger ringing in our ears, we arrived at the appointed time in the evening and were met by an armed security guard who ushered us through an iron gate. Our identities were checked and we were led on into the villa. From there another member of Amin's household took us on into the drawing room where we waited for the former tyrant. He soon appeared and received us warmly as was his way on such occasions. Shaking hands he appeared to be in a jovial mood, as ever, and was remarkably the same physically as I remembered him from fourteen years earlier.

The drawing room was modestly furnished. He offered us some soft drinks, and at first our conversation was limited to pleasantries. I addressed him as Mr.

President as I had done in our past meetings in Uganda and asked him how he and his family were getting on in Saudi Arabia. For a while he was somewhat guarded as he seemed to spar with us, trying to gauge our intentions and detect any possible ulterior motive in our meeting. Once he was satisfied that we were in no way spying nor did we pose any threat, he warmed up and the atmosphere became very relaxed. We spoke a lot about the situation and history of Uganda, but he was equally interested in the political landscape of Britain and listened carefully to my comments and observations. The time went by quickly and we had in fact stayed much longer than we had planned. As we began to take our leave around 10 o'clock, Amin, enjoying himself thoroughly by now, holding court and discussing affairs close to his heart, insisted we stay for dinner. We could not of course decline and were in any case obviously keen to spend more time in the company of this singular man. Other members of his group living in Jeddah, including one General Bashir, his Prime Minister in waiting, were summoned by telephone and they soon joined us, swelling our numbers even further as by now we had already been joined by some of his family.

We were served a lavish meal prepared by Amin's wife over the next two hours and we continued an interesting and insightful conversation. I found that not only was Amin well informed about the situation in Uganda but that he also had a thorough grasp of the international political scene and was particularly unhappy with America's treatment of his friend Colonel Gaddafi.

He told me of his hopes of returning to power in Uganda and secret visits to Sudan and Zaire to assess his support, and he assured me repeatedly that if he ever got another opportunity he would do great things for Uganda and its people. (He did in fact attempt his return to Uganda in 1989 through Kinshasa to lead an armed group, but was unsuccessful.)

On the issue of his expulsion of the Asians from Uganda he urged me repeatedly to advise former Ugandan Asians to return to Uganda and restart their businesses. This was his way of acknowledging the grave economic blow he had dealt the country in expelling the Asian community, the backbone of the country's prosperity, so hastily and unceremoniously.

Eventually, sometime after midnight, we began to leave. On our way out Amin showed us a blackboard in an adjoining room on which were scribbled some German words. He told us that he was learning the German language from a German teacher, remaining still a great admirer of Hitler and certain elements of German culture. He walked with us outside the villa and showed us on the way the Ugandan matoke (plantain) tree and the mohogo (cassava) plants that he had grown in his garden that he had brought with him when he fled the country in 1979. As we reached our car, parked just outside his gate, he embraced us warmly before bidding goodbye. We shook hands and parted. The difference this time was that he was no longer dangerous behind all his charm because he no longer had any power, and I was no longer perceived as an enemy and no longer on his hit list, though I knew the truth of so much that had happened during his rule and rise to power.

Shortly thereafter, though much later than we had planned, we returned to our thoroughly worried wives.

That was the last time I met Idi Amin. He lived to be an apparently sprightly eighty year old without ever having been brought to justice for the crimes he committed. Three decades after first meeting him I have neither feelings of hatred towards Amin for what he did to me and my family, nor of any joy at his demise.

Printed in Great Britain
by Amazon